ENLIGHTENMENT
IS SEXY

EVERY WOMAN'S GUIDE TO A
MAGICAL LIFE

VALERIE GANGAS

18 17 16 15 14 13   10 9 8 7 6 5 4 3 2 1

Enlightenment is Sexy
ISBN: 978-0-9963502-5-9
Copyright © 2015 by Valerie Gangas

Cover by George Foster, fostercovers.com

In 2011, I *woke up* and realized everything I thought I knew was wrong."
– Valerie Gangas

TABLE OF CONTENTS

Introduction: Enlightenment Is Sexy 7

Chapter 1 17
Once Upon a Time...My Back Story:
How my Spiritual Doors Got Blown Wide Open

Chapter 2 29
You Are Not in Control: Trust Me

Chapter 3 39
Love is in the Air: Don't Settle

Chapter 4 49
Follow the Signs: Your Soul Already Knows

Chapter 5 63
Everyone You Meet is a Mirror

Chapter 6 71
Emotional Vampires

Chapter 7 85
Don't Fit In

Chapter 8 95
Stop Being Married to the Results

Chapter 9 105
Write it Down and Make it Your Reality

Chapter 10 113
Stepping Into Your Dreams

Chapter 11 123
The Underestimated Power of Simplicity

Chapter 12 131
Set Yourself Free With Forgiveness

Chapter 13 139
Thinking is Overrated:
Escape Your Mental Prison

Chapter 14 151
Becoming a Master at Manifesting

Chapter 15 161
Seek Truth in Meditation

Chapter 16 171
Destroy What No Longer Works for You

Chapter 17 181
Signs of a Spiritual Awakening

Chapter 18 191
I Know What Sadness Is: Getting Perspective on
Grief and Loss

Chapter 19 201
Experience is Your Best Teacher

Chapter 20 211
What To Do When the World Doesn't Get You

Chapter 21 221
The Misunderstood Power of Prayer

Open Letter To You, Dear Reader 229

Dedication & Acknowledgment 233

Introduction

Enlightenment
Is Sexy

"Be who God meant you to be
and you will set the world on fire"

—*St. Catherine of Siena (14th cent.)*

Ladies, isn't it true? We spend so much time reading fashion magazines or gossip magazines, constantly looking for the latest trend or the hottest style. And as soon as we buy a new pair of leather pants, cropped jeans are in! Red lipstick is popular one month and the next month it's nude lip gloss; waif models in the 90's, Kate Upton and her curves in 2015. Who are our role models, the *Kardashians*?

Have you noticed where all of this nonsense has gotten you? A one-way ticket to a life of subtle self-loathing. That's right, you've been cleverly ushered into the "I suck" zone. *Lose 10 pounds in 10 days! Get a flawless face, fast! Who wore it best?* I mean, give me a break! These tips of the trade are no *tips* at all. Their content is insensitive, confusing and based on a conception of you as a thing to be molded (into a specific image), rather than a person who's already perfection incarnate. It's as though they're all saying, "You'll begin living the magical life *if you just lose a few pounds!*" By seducing you into focusing on what *they* (the media, advertisers, "normal" society) want you to pay attention to—some supposedly more ideal future—they're steering you away from your true self, away from living contentedly in the present. It makes us women feel like we aren't good enough unless we're a size zero with porcelain skin. *I* ask, "Good enough for *whom*? A boyfriend who's superficial and only cares about your looks? A mother who wants you to look and act like a Southern pageant queen? Who exactly are we torturing ourselves for and why won't it stop?"

What if I was to tell you that most everything you've been focusing on—regarding "who you are"—is complete bullshit, that the media and anything or anyone else trying to put artificial standards on you is false, and the people around you who buy into it are actually contributing to the problem? It's hard to conceive the entire world is in on this nasty joke. What I've come to realize is they are, and yet they aren't. See, everyone is just feeding into the same machine—the machine that is *outside* of yourself. The machine that fuels the false belief "looking good equals feeling good," or that bit about perfect grades in school guaranteeing you a perfect life or that the "right" job will buy your happiness. In a world where self-help books are flying off the shelves and AA meetings are busting at the seams, I took a look around and found myself asking, "What the hell is going on?!"

It seems to me that we as a society—especially us women—often feel out of control and totally overwhelmed. And as much as we try, no amount of partying, different boyfriends or large paychecks is going to solve this issue. The problem seems to boil down to this: *We are looking outside ourselves to solve our problems.*

That approach, my friends, does not work. *Not at all.* But no one tells you that little secret! The advice you usually hear is to get a prescription, buy yourself a new outfit and just lose 15 more pounds . . . and before you know it, you'll feel more like "yourself."

But who is this "yourself" character we are talking about?

This is the question with which you need to begin to lay the foundation for the rest of your life. Who are you? Do you even know? Pretty scary stuff. Hang with me for a minute, though. What do you think would happen if you really took the time and space to be able to truly answer that question? Do you think it would change the way you look at things and what you would accept as being cool with you? How you would spend your time? If you could just answer that one question, trust me, your whole life would change.

Do you believe beauty comes from within . . . or do you think that's something your mom tells you, well, because she's your mom? Get this—it's actually true. Everything, in fact, that happens in your life comes from *inside of you*. No one else, only *you*. Learn it, live it and embrace it. No one else is creating your reality. So, if your life sucks, you know who to go after. You keep getting screamed at by your boss? Pay attention, you're in the *wrong job*. (Start thinking of what you'd *really* like to be doing for work.) Can't lose a pound, even though you work out 3 hours a day? You might be holding on to the weight for protection. You work your ass off, but don't have a dollar to show for it? Um, Houston, we have a problem. That's right . . . an "inside" problem.

You can keep truckin' along with things as they are, but one day you are going to get slammed. You might get fired, you might get dumped, hell, you might even get evicted. One way or another, the laws of nature are going to catch up with you. And *then* you'll pay attention to your life with the laser focus of a surgeon. What we're trying to do is get to you *before* you hit that point . . . because otherwise, it's not going to be pretty.

Right about now, you might be asking, "So, what qualifies *you* to be throwing out 'self-help' advice like beaded necklaces off a Mardi Gras float?"

As a matter of fact, embedded into the rest of this book is my response to that question . . . and in a nutshell, my answer amounts to this: In *Enlightenment is Sexy*, I don't talk about anything I haven't experienced, learned or discovered for myself. That is, my life experiences have led me to understand everything I share in this book. The "principles," "rules of the road" and "universal laws" I'll be telling you about are certainly not new, but my take on them is derived from my own personal journey of awakening. And in each chapter, whenever I'm pointing something out to you or suggesting you look at something a particular way, I'll be sharing with you at least one anecdote (if not more) from my own life that contributed to my "getting" what I'm hoping you'll "get" too!

Now, if you "get" that you, your thoughts and your beliefs play a major part in creating your reality, my question for you is this: What are you going to do about it? Obviously you have to help yourself, which means really getting to the root of whatever's keeping you stuck in one area of your life or another. And let me be clear with you – identifying the obstacles isn't always easy, and neither is getting rid of them or replacing them. Typically, you've been carrying them around for a long time and they're "comfortable" where they are (hence, the term "comfort zone"—which you need to get *out* of in order to grow or allow change to happen!). But the choice is yours to stay stuck or to get up and get going with this opportunity to recreate your reality.

If you choose the latter, you can start by re-directing your attention *away* from other people's business and onto what's going on with *you*. For example, you could start spending more time with the TV turned off. (Most of it is likely just filling your mind with more false beliefs and making the unconscious ones you have grow.) The same goes for gossip websites. (I mean, what *are* the benefits to be had from following Perez Hilton and TMZ, anyway?) And unless fashion is your life, put away the *Glamour* magazine and figure out what "sexy" means to *you*!

There is a *whole world* inside of you waiting to be tapped into. Once I began paying attention to what was going on within my own inner world, some pretty radical change started occurring. In the midst of my telling you about what I experienced and what I chose to do with what I observed—to live differently than I had in the past—I'll share with you what became clear to me in the process. Fundamentally, this book is aimed at showing you how to create lasting, positive, kick-ass change in your life . . . and ultimately, it's about how to lead an enlightened, magical life! *BOOM!*

The bottom line is this: Wouldn't it be amazing to have such a strong sense of self that you effortlessly attract the perfect partner, an amazing job or whatever it is your heart has longed for, but has eluded you for what seems like your whole life? And what if that same, well-developed sense of who you are would naturally bring you more happiness than you ever dreamed of? Sign me up for that one! And get this: *All* of that is not only possible, it's your *birthright*.

"Okay," you might be saying to yourself, "that sounds good, but what about this 'enlightenment' you've included in your book's title? How does *that* fit in here?" Good question! For me, 'enlightenment' refers to the most well-developed sense of who you are. Period. No filters or veils over your eyes about your true nature. No limiting beliefs. In fact, it's not a *belief* that divinity lies within all of life . . . it is a personal experience of this. It's the actual experience of the Universe dwelling in all life. Hence, enlightenment is not a theory . . . it's a *knowing*. You are living it, because it is unwavering at the core of your being.

So when you *are* living a life of increasing enlightenment, you're naturally experiencing more of what *really* is available to you—the gifts of the Universe make their way to your doorstep more easily (without your self-made obstacles holding them forever at arm's length), and your desires are met with fulfillment more readily (any conscious or unconscious resistances to receiving and tendencies to self-sabotage having been quelled).

The question is when and how you are going to claim this "magical life" for yourself. As for the "when," you can start now, by reading onward *and* by choosing to make any "behavior adjustments" you feel inspired to make along the way.

As for the "how," well, after you turn off *The Bachelor*, you can focus on the most interesting topic going—*yourself*. In *Enlightenment is Sexy*, you'll be shown exactly what you need to do to have a truly extraordinary life *on your terms*. You heard it correctly, *your* terms—not your parents', society's or your friends'. It's all you, babe. You have all the power you need to create the life you have always dreamed of. I have been exactly where you are and fought the good fight. I came out on the other side and created a life of magic, wonder, synchronicity and excitement for myself, which has given me plenty of stories to tell (you'll find those nestled in the pages to come). I can tell you right now, *this* is the only way to roll.

But just like I had to figure out that *I* was responsible for my happiness and that it's an "inside job," so must you have the courage to face up to the fact that it's *your* story—that it's up to *you* to take the reins and write it the way *you* want it. With the right tools, you will be unstoppable. Crying on a Saturday night while eating a whole pizza will be some *other* girl's reality. You'll be too busy making your mark on the world and having a blast!

1

Once Upon a Time...

My Back Story: How my Spiritual Doors Got Blown Wide Open

This is who we really are. We are one blink of an eye away from being fully awake."

—*Pema Chodron*

For as long as I can remember, my journey through life has taught me not to get attached to "one way" of seeing or doing things *and* that I'm wisest when I maintain an openness to new perspectives on everything, *including* myself. One lesson I've learned is that whatever I'm carrying—be it a belief about myself or the world, an expectation of others, anything at all—can be a gift or a curse, depending on a variety of factors.

In my case, ever since I was young, I was what many people call an *empath*—that is, I could clearly feel people's emotions, especially their pain, and I would often sense their thoughts as well. Having this ability was not always a blessing, though. At an early age, it could get so intense that there were days I would come home from school and just cry for hours. Yeah, I had a bunch of friends with whom I spent my time, but everything was far from being a bed of roses. As I got older, this hyper-receptive inner world of mine became so heavy-duty at times, I often thought I was going mad. In fact, when I was sixteen, I told my mom I was "hearing voices," which I've come to find out were actually thoughts travelling from other people's minds to mine. I mean, other people's thoughts were dropping like parachutes into my brain and I could not figure out what the hell was happening!

It was only by the grace of God that I eventually ended up with a psychologist—my mom's doctor, actually—who was somewhat of an expert in this field. Not only was he interested in the psychic phenomena I'd experienced from an early age, but he also had other clients who were having the same kind of experiences as me. Just the fact that he told me there were other people in the world just like me helped me tremendously. Everything that was taking place in my life was "real" to me, of course, but *he* recognized it as such and confirmed it for me. Over time, this kind, keenly insightful doctor taught me simple techniques to help protect myself and "hold on to my energy." One day, he finally put a name to who I was: "Valerie, you are a *highly* sensitive person."

I felt so thankful this particular doctor helped me as much as he did, but other than him and my mom, I didn't feel like anyone could really "see" me. This still bothered me, leaving me confused and at times depressed. And because I didn't have anyone on the "outside" to talk to at the time, I simply tried to numb myself from these experiences by going out all the time, partying, always having a boyfriend and constantly doing something. *Anything.* This pattern would continue until I was thirty-four years old.

After helping out and supporting my mom as best as I could for thirteen years while she battled with cancer, when she passed away I was a major train wreck—deep depression, suicidal thoughts and countless nights of insomnia were just a few of my "symptoms." A few months later, when a friend suggested I learn to meditate, my only hope was that I would be able to get some sleep. I hadn't read anything about meditation, hadn't thought about it or even wondered about it. But I was in such a dark place after my mother's death, one morning, I made the call.

Within days, off I went to a Transcendental Meditation center in Chicago. The home which doubled as a "TM" center had a feeling of calm I couldn't quite put my finger on—the air seemed lighter, somehow, and the view was all lake. Even upon entering the center's lobby, I felt a bit calmer. *Huh,* I thought, *these people who work here are super different.* They were so chilled and completely filled with love, it was immediately clear to me they were there to help me. My next thought was, *I'm here, so I might as well learn how to do this.*

I sat down with my teacher and after a short, but beautiful Indian ceremony, I was given my "mantra"—a sound that she said my awareness would naturally follow as it subsided into the depths of silence in my mind. When we both closed our eyes, I easily and effortlessly said the mantra to myself less than five times . . . and just like that, *I was gone.* I dove into a part of my body and mind I never knew existed—boundless, limitless and totally awesome. Something major had just happened and I was about to find out what it was.

As I got in my car to drive home, I began flying down Lake Shore Drive, immediately noticing how the world seemed so much different to me than it did on my way *to* the center. The colors were more vivid, the sounds of the birds felt like sweet music to my ears, the trees seemed to be connected to me and above all, I felt happy. *But,* my mind called out to me, *Is this really happening?! Do I really feel happy? How? Why? What the hell?* Luckily, the essence of that experience stuck and stayed, and I came to find that it *was* in fact "real"—that in twenty minutes, *my whole life had changed.* I *woke up* and realized everything I thought I knew was wrong. My life was no longer defined by outer circumstances. I was having a direct experience of what I have come to know as my true Self.

It took me a couple of weeks to adjust to this new feeling, but *man*, it was incredible. Now, looking back, I would say my experience of learning to do TM was nothing short of miraculous. (In fact, my 13-year-long sleeping problem just disappeared after my first meditation!)

Fast-forward a couple of months and I was meditating every day, feeling stronger, clearer and more conscious, week-by-week. I noticed most everything seemed easier and synchronicity had begun making regular appearances in my life. For example, I had the thought, *I really need a new car, but I don't have a ton of cash.* Within 24 hours, one of my best girlfriends called me and asked if I wanted her old BMW. I couldn't believe it! She said her dad was sick of looking at it sitting in the driveway and he didn't feel like taking the time to sell it. I bought it from her for $1 a day later, and I wondered, *Does this happen to other people, or am I just an ecstatic alien?*

The mind-blower was it had only been a short time before starting to meditate that I had been planning to give away my dog, give away all my belongings and *end my life.* My relationship with my mom had been so close and so beautiful that after she died, I saw no point in living. I'd continually thought, *How can I go on without her?* It didn't seem possible. I'd sobbed and wailed myself to sleep, night after night, desperately praying for a solution to my grief and an end to the deeply dark sadness in my soul. I *never* could have guessed it would come in the form of something as simple as meditation. You know what they say, though: "Be careful what you wish for, 'cause you just might get it." Well, I was about to "get it" and in a *big* way.

One Saturday night, about six months after my mom had died, I had a ticket to go see one of my favorite musicians, Sade. She never seems to tour, so I figured this show was going to be epic. At the same time, a friend who I had not seen in twenty years called to tell me he was in town (Chicago). He wanted to know if I would be interested in having dinner with him and the Foo Fighters and then going to an intimate show they were doing later in the evening. I promptly said, "No, I've got plans already and I don't even know any of their music." I know it sounds crazy that I turned down dinner with the Foo Fighters, but for some unexplainable reason I just didn't care.

Well, this kid must have been dying to see me, because he sent me fifty text messages over the course of the evening and eventually broke me down. After seeing Sade perform, I showed up at midnight to the show and, just as he'd promised, I was whisked up to the VIP section of the venue. I looked around and saw so many famous people, I stopped counting after a while. *This is interesting,* I thought, *How the hell did I end up here?* The show was amazing, but the *really* good stuff was about to get rolling.

After the show ended at around 2:30 a.m., we were talking a bit and just waiting around to go backstage. I looked over my shoulder, only to see this huge mound of red hair coming up the stairs. I remember thinking, *Well, this person coming up really missed the boat—the show is already over!* As I looked closer, it was Wynonna Judd! *Holy Shit! What is Wynonna Judd doing at a Foo Fighters show?!*

Now, I need to share with you a brief interlude that relates to what happened next. I hadn't told anyone, but I had been offered a job working with

Oprah Winfrey and Rosie O'Donnell to help out as their entire staffs learned how to meditate. I'd had such a great experience with Transcendental Meditation that when Oprah came calling to the TM people in Chicago, they figured I would be the perfect girl to bring onto the team as a sort of spokesperson. As far as the Chicago TM teachers were concerned, I was a regular, fun-loving, easy-breezy kind of girl with a gift for connecting with people *and* I'd be a natural at sharing about the benefits of learning meditation. When they approached me about it, I felt appreciative of their offer, but I turned the job down. I mean, in my mind I thought, *What am I going to tell Oprah that she doesn't already know?* "No way," I said. "I'm not interested."

Now, I know what you're probably thinking. *What out-of-work girl in her thirties turns down a job working with Oprah?* Well, *this* girl. But here's some *more* background stuff. For years, my mom had been obsessed with a performance Wynonna Judd had done on *The Oprah Show* of the Foreigner song, "I Want to Know What Love Is" (Wynonna *had* passionately knocked a home run with it). I mean, Mom seemed to always have that CD in her car stereo, and I'd regularly hear her singing along to it. Well, when my mom was in the middle of chemo treatments and all she could really do was take it easy and watch a little TV, she chose to watch *Wynonna's* performance of that tune—sometimes *continually,* over and over—and I couldn't help but tease her about it. What I'm trying to point out is this: If there was one person on Earth who it was going to shock me to meet, Wynonna Judd was that person.

To take this story to an even crazier level, before my mom passed away, I had a long talk with her about trying to keep in touch with me from the "other" side. I gave her strict orders to do everything in her power to contact me. I even suggested she do it through music and that I would be watching for it. Well, she obviously wasn't messing around! She brought me the actual artist. Sounds like my mom.

You think that's all? The guy who I was with at the show *just happened to know Wynonna*. So, within seconds, the three of us were sitting there talking about, well, life! And after a couple minutes of yakking away, I just busted out, "I have to tell you something, Wynonna!"

She looked at me and said, "Alright, shoot."

I told her the story about my mom and how the performance she'd done on *Oprah* had boosted my mom's spirits. I even told her how I had just been offered this job to help teach Oprah and her staff to meditate. I told her I'd said no, at which point I just looked at her thinking, *I might have made a mistake*.

She took my hand and said, "Honey, you go take that job for your mom and you show them who you are: *a child of God*."

Holy Christ. I had always told myself, secretly, when things got really bad, "I am a child of God" and that I was protected. I wondered, *Is Wynonna Judd channeling my mom?*

Next thing I knew, we were shuffling down the stairs to go hang backstage with the band. All the Foo Fighters were super-cool and very laid back. We hung out, ate pizza and talked about the show. Within 15 minutes, the guys in the band invited me to come to Lollapalooza the next day and watch the show from the stage. This was all so bizarre, I just decided to roll with it. I replied, "Sure, why not?"

The next day, everything happened exactly as they said it would. I was given free tickets, a backstage pass and a third pass into an "Artists" section. My mind was reeling. *So, this is how it goes when you feel good?* About thirty minutes before the show, I was on the stage next to the band and it started raining cats and dogs, as though a monsoon had kicked up! I looked around only to see I was surrounded by celebrities, including one of my favorite people ever, Anthony Bourdain (the world famous chef). *Now,* I thought, *this is getting interesting.*

The show started and I looked out at thousands of screaming fans getting their asses kicked by rain with the entire Chicago skyline rearing up into the space behind them. The energy on the stage was electrifying, and suddenly I realized I had crossed over into another dimension of life.

Everything was alive, powerful and beyond exciting. My world was turning into something beyond my wildest dreams and all I had done was become quiet through a simple form of meditation. Dig it, *that's* some powerful stuff.

By that Friday morning, I was standing in a screening room with Oprah Winfrey and Sheri Salata (President of Oprah's Harpo Productions), telling them how meditating was going to change their lives. I looked Oprah in the eye and told her that her life was going to become boundless, limitless and she was going to be happier than she could ever imagine. She looked at Sheri, her right-hand woman, and simply said, "I want what that girl has."

I meant every word I said to her. I had no fear, and Oprah didn't feel any different to me than a friend or any other person I cared about. We were all the same at the core and I knew it. My life changed in that moment, and it was clear to me I had been put on this earth to help people. I felt I had been reborn with knowledge I can only describe as coming from "a higher power." I realized this isn't something any of us can learn in a classroom—it's something we can only experience. And upon experiencing it for the first time, the world became so beautiful that all I could feel was joy and gratitude for simply having been born.

It was *then* I knew this thing was real and it was going to be an *amazing* ride.

2 You Are Not in Control— Trust Me

"Let us liberate ourselves from any form of control. Let us focus at the inner drum, where the rhythm aligns with that of our heart."

—*Grigoris Deoudis*

We seem to love control, yet do we ever really *have* it? When I realistically examine two of the major categories of my life—people (including their attitudes and behaviors) and the countless, ever-changing situations I encounter on a daily basis—I get a not-so-gentle reminder that I'm hardly *ever* in control of anything outside of me. However, I'd say finding the wherewithal to accept that lack of control as a "fact of life" is not on most people's daily agendas—nor is humbling ourselves in the face of such a challenge.

In other words, most people find it's *not* easy-peasy doing what the Serenity Prayer1 suggests, "...accept the things I cannot change...." Instead (at least in my case), I look at my circumstances and ask, "If I can't control 'x', then where *can* I find joy? Where *can* I find happiness?"

Interestingly enough, facing major life events has taught me something about that question. I've found that "accepting" my inability to control the outcome of any situation *can* feel pretty damn overwhelming—to the point where I've actually felt I was in hell. However, by consciously and intentionally opening my mind and heart to simply *accepting the situation* right there in the moment, to surrendering to "what is," I *have* discovered it's possible to find

---

1 Serenity Prayer: "God, grant me the serenity to accept the things I cannot change, the courage to change the things I can, and the wisdom to know the difference." – Reinhold Niebuhr

peace *despite the problem*. Ultimately, it comes down to choosing where I put my attention (in this case, my acceptance), because *that* is what will grow.

My mom always told me that when I gave up the belief that tells me, "I need to have everything a certain way to be happy," my life would naturally expand and start including even greater possibilities. I never understood what she meant . . . until I actually began experiencing it myself. And let me tell you, she was *so* right. I mean, she nailed it.

At one point, what I had *previously* imagined for my life *had* come to pass—owning my own restaurant, varying levels of relationships with handsome, successful alpha males, big portions of travel and adventure—but they all had been projections of what I *thought* would make me happy, which was tied to my secret longing to control how everything went. It's like I'd concluded *I* knew what was best for me . . . and I didn't need (or have time for) life/the Universe/ God to show me what was truly in store for me and my happiness. "Nope, thank you very much, I've got that covered! Everything's under (my) control."

But when my mother passed away, I got a crash course in understanding there was a whole lot I just couldn't control—and my relatively limited imagination was miniscule in comparison to what the Universe could muster.

When I look back at that time, I "get" I was at the turning point, at the very end of my rope. I mean, my mom—my best friend in the world—had passed away from a long bout with cancer and I had been a grieving train wreck for months. Uncertain whether or not I wanted to die, but fairly certain I didn't want to live, I barely grasped that rope in my trembling hands. The way I saw my circumstances, I could either off myself or I could receive a miracle. I saw no other choice.

One day in the shower, I completely broke down and surrendered. I abandoned everything I knew and just prayed. I prayed like my life depended on it, because it *did*. I could no longer handle my world, so I had no choice but to give it up.

I gave up the illusion *I* was in control, that *I* was making everything happen and that *I* didn't need any help. In truth, I needed more help at that moment than at any other time in my entire life. Looking back, I can see how important this breakdown was in determining my next steps. I believe that God, the Universe, a "higher power," nudged me to the edge of a cliff to break down the "know-it-all control freak" in me. It worked—I surrendered completely—and I don't believe any-thing else would have, because I was a wild, cocky girl who didn't want to listen to anyone. I thought I had *all* the answers. What a joke! In reality, I knew next to nothing.

Immediately, as I started down my new path—a road that reminded me *daily* I could *not* control people, events and outcomes the way I'd formerly thought I could—I had to learn to *trust*. Rather quickly, in fact, my faith was tested in a big way.

Two months after my mother passed away, one of my close friends—Linda—and her friend who had lost her son to suicide a couple years prior went to see a highly regarded "spirit medium" named Mollie. (Neither of them had had any experience with mediums, psychics or anything else in that realm.) I learned later from Linda that they sat in a room with this very normal-looking woman, and she began to tell both of them things she *never* could have known in any way, shape or form: intimate details about both Linda's father, who had passed away a couple years earlier, and about her friend's son.

Upon her return, Linda immediately called me. "Val, you *have* to call this lady, Mollie. She can completely talk to dead people!"

Without hesitating, I said, "Alright, I'll call her." I made an appointment and a week later was on Skype with Mollie, a quite pretty, 30-something woman with kindness spilling out of her eyes. I instantly felt safe, fully trusting I was in good hands. Within one minute of starting, my mom "came through." In fact, the medium said my mom nearly knocked her over trying to get to me. Mollie described my mother perfectly—a gypsy woman with a long flowing black skirt, big hair and large gold earrings. She also said my mom was so thrilled to connect with me, she began dancing and twirling like a whirling dervish. I thought, *Yep, that's my mom.*

In the next breath, Mollie said, "You need to take care of Jim." Jim was my mom's brother. She went on to explain he would become ill shortly thereafter and my mom was asking me to take care of him.

My head was spinning. This family member who I loved deeply was evidently going to get sick. *But when? Why? How could I help him?* If I were planning on killing myself, how in God's name would I have the strength to help anyone else? Nevertheless, the medium was adamant I *must* do this.

Mollie also told me my mother said I was going to change careers, showing her a vision of me going up an escalator that seemed to take me all the way up to heaven. She went on to say my life was going to take a huge turn—that I was very much needed on earth.

Within a few months, I *had* become a completely different person—strong, fearless and deeply spiritual. I had learned to meditate, and I became increasingly intuitive, welcoming answers as they came to me. And as time went on, I kind of forgot about this session with the medium.

But wouldn't you know it, very soon (three months later), Uncle Jim, who my mom had named, became very ill and ended up in the hospital. I was always extremely close with him, as he was the rebel of the family—I could so easily relate to him, in that regard—and we'd naturally connected from when I was young. He'd always told me the same thing: "Val, don't ask permission. Don't tell people what you are going to do. Just go do it. Have your own experiences on your *own* terms." A strong-minded, skydiving, brilliant pilot uncle, he was all I had left from my mom's immediate family.

When he started to become really ill, he confided in me that, since my mom was gone and he had lost most of his friends, he was ready to move on. I knew what this meant: he was going to leave this earth. And in that moment, I decided I was going to be with him as much as possible. I let go and surrendered to the reality that I was going to lose him . . . and I understood that, just like life had shown me, nothing and no one was going to control my uncle.

This would become one of the most powerful lessons I would ever learn.

Since my mom had asked me to take care of him, I was determined to do whatever it took to carry out her wishes. I began regularly driving down to Tennessee from Chicago to just sit with him. Finally, at one point, he told me he was getting ready to check out. I didn't try to change his mind. We would talk for hours, and all the while, I just kept accepting the fact he was dying. The weird part was, because I had released all control and just lived in the present moment with my uncle, I started to experience happiness with him. It sounds strange, but even in his death, I felt an extraordinary sense of love and happiness. I saw the beauty in an action that, years before, would have absolutely destroyed me. He fearlessly let his faith carry him through, and I was lucky to ride along with him. It showed me *my* new-found faith in letting go was serving me. Day by day, I was learning to trust God.

Just like my mom had done, my uncle took me by the hand and showed me how to die *before* I died,—but this time I was composed, solidly connected with the Universe and certain that everything was okay. I was unshakeable.

Uncle Jim eventually passed away and I was there to wrap my arms around my cousins and my aunt, to love them and pray with them, all the while hearing my mom's words, "Take care of Jim."

At this point, it was clear to me I had truly surrendered "control" to a higher power. I had opened up (and not held tightly to "comfort zone" beliefs) in order to really listen to my mother's words expressed through Mollie. And I had let God carry out the end of my uncle's life, instead of fighting it.

As for that vision of me taking an escalator up towards the heavens? It was happening. To some real measure, I *had* "risen up" and aligned myself with the Universe in a better, less stressful and less controlling way.

My mom's message led me to practice having faith and trust, even in the midst of difficult and confusing times. Ultimately, I realized I *am* needed here on this earth, even if I occasionally question my purpose.

But above all, she helped me learn how to surrender to life, death and everything in between. She helped me figure out I'm not in control of so-o-o much—and that it's okay. In fact, it's perfect.

As you begin to give up the delusion *you* are running the show, you start feeling a sense of freedom that leads straight to faith's doorstep. And combining faith with meditation or prayer eventually leads you to an authentic connection with your higher self, which naturally brings about a "super-intuition" that can be a tremendous guide for every decision and choice you face.

My experience has shown me that the "inside information" I receive when I meditate or simply pay attention to my gut resembles a sort of benevolent map: *Turn left, call this person, travel to a different state, read this book* . . . and it never ends.

This more "plugged in" state of consciousness provides us with a smooth, steady stream of "inside information" that leads into the heart of life's boldest, brightest, most wondrous existence.

Once you are tapped into this flow, life becomes magical, which is how we are meant to be living. (No, life is *not* supposed to be insanely difficult.) The voice and guiding hand is there for all of us should we choose to tune in and listen. Remember, it *is* our birthright.

ENLIGHTENMENT IS SEXY CHAPTER TOOLBOX

You Are Not In Control

Release control, gain freedom. Giving up control sets you up to gain something greater.

Pay attention to your gut. It never lies to you (but your ego does).

Open your eyes (and your mind)! The Universe has way bigger plans for you . . . starting *now!*

3

Love is in the Air– Don't Settle

"The biggest human temptation is to settle for too little."

—*Thomas Merton*

The old saying, "You can't have true love till you truly love yourself," is probably still around because it's dead-on right. When I look at the increasing way "long-lasting" marriages and relationships are viewed with awe and wonder (rather than seen as "par for the course"), and the vast number of women who seem to "settle for less" when it comes to relationships, I wonder why we—as a society—were never taught the value of this principle to begin with.

Once upon a time, I seemed to always be in a relationship, going from one to another (usually lasting between 3 – 5 years), ending when I could no longer ignore I was with the wrong guy. Don't get me wrong, the men I dated were all pretty exceptional people, and I usually felt fortunate to be with them and loved by them. It's just that, I typically could tell things weren't really "meant to be" between me and Mr. X . . . but "settling for less" just seemed to be part of the game. I mean, I liked guys and they liked me . . . and it just seemed so natural for me to be in a relationship, even if I knew "he" was not what I was truly looking for.

If you can relate with this, then you'll likely also recognize that the Universe/God—always supportive of our growth and expansion—will eventually step in, put something smack-dab in front of us to get our attention, and point us in a new, healthier direction . . . right? We just need to be alert to the signals and respond to the call!

In my case, my mom passed away, and I felt *no* desire to be in a relationship, longing instead for solitude and time to reflect on who I am and what I *really* want to be doing with my time on Earth. However, there are *countless* life events and circumstances that can arise to remind you it's time you do a "reality check" on yourself and whatever relationship you're in. From losing a job to being promoted, from a change of residence to an unexpected health issue, whatever it takes for you to look more deeply into the mirror, Life itself will nudge you into accepting that a change of some sort is being called for. That is, *if* you are no longer willing to put up with the pain, the runaround, the self-loathing many of us experience when you settle for less. Ultimately, the Universe will "persuade" each of us to see what we're really doing to ourselves by staying in this or that relationship.

If you have been thrust into a situation or find yourself desiring a life without this or that person who has been a dominant part of your day-to-day existence (for better or for worse), new questions begin to emerge. I strongly suggest you give yourself some time and answer these questions like it matters, *because it does!*:

How do I want to live?
Who am I here to be?
What values are important to me?
How am I going to help others?

For me, doing a top-to-bottom evaluation of myself, by asking and sincerely answering questions like these, caused me to get honest about "where I was at" and in which direction I *really* wanted to move. Eventually, I turned to the spiritual side of myself both for guidance and to empower me to follow that guidance.

Once again, there are many different ways and approaches to getting in touch with your spiritual side, when you're seeking insight and inspiration regarding where and how "love" best fits into your life: prayer, meditation, yoga, art, music, walking, backpacking in nature . . . the list could go on. The important thing is to choose something you feel aligned with and capable of doing regularly, something you feel naturally drawn to, even if there's an initial unfamiliarity or "anxiety over the details" ("Do I need a yoga mat?" "Is it kosher to hike in tennis shoes?" etc.) And don't worry about the results! (Leave those to God/the Universe.) At this point, your job is simple: identify what feels right for you and then, as the Nike ad says, 'Just do it!'

Myself, I chose to jump off the high dive right into the deep end of *my soul*. I learned to meditate and everything shifted pretty rapidly. Seemingly overnight, I felt a profound connection with the world, a huge leap forward in my sense of intimacy with the Universe, and I realized that God actually *is* in everything around me, including myself.

So, when I'd be approached by a guy lining me up in his sights, I began responding from a different place than I had in the past: what I'd say or do was now based on whether or not I sensed it felt right to my soul, my gut. Period.

Match.com? Are you serious? What planet are all these people living on? I don't have time for that! I'm getting juiced up exploring the nature of my existence.

The bottom line? I've learned more from *not* dating than I ever did from continuously being attached. In fact, not dating was one of the best decisions I ever made.

That being said, were there days when I felt concerned by my lack of interest in dating? Of course. But at the same time, after years of being in relationships, it also felt pretty awesome. It was different, but not in a bad way. It gave me the chance to take a breather and redirect my life.

And it may well be that, from time to time, many women (you included?) need that breather, that redirect. Ultimately, you need to be the one to decide what's right and best for you.

Certainly, adjusting to this "focused on myself" lifestyle *will* feel new to you. For once, you won't have to check in with anyone. Gone will be the days when you worry about what you're going to make for dinner or if you can hang out with your girlfriends on a Saturday night. No need for a second opinion.

In other words, you actually *can* roam the earth at will without someone else's seal of approval.

It is all up to you. You, alone, are free to write the next chapter in the story of your life. How liberating! *Freedom*—freedom like you may have never tasted it before.

Over the past couple of years, operating with this new paradigm in place, I have come to understand exactly who I am: a child of God . . . a woman with a deep longing to make her mark on the world, to connect with people, and above all, to be kind.

I started a company I love, advanced my daily meditation practice (which is the backbone of my existence), road-tripped all over the country, wrote this book, realized my love of skydiving and met a group of people who I consider to be my soul family. I finally became the person I always wanted to be . . . I became whole.

Prior to my inner pilgrimage, it felt like I was just spinning my wheels. I was generally a happy camper, but often enough, a bit confused. I knew there was more to life, but I just couldn't get there. It was out of my reach. Now, though, I feel more distinct, fulfilled and happy — a wonderful combo platter.

Ultimately, as a result of my introspective time spent not dating, I figured out the best way (at least for me) to enter into a meaningful relationship: *be the love you want; be the person you want to meet.*

There is no point getting involved with another human if we need them to "complete" us. That is a recipe for emptiness, confusion and disaster. We are *already* complete. We just have to open our minds and souls to see it. It's right there, inside of all of us.

The key is you have to experience it for yourself, not just read about it. You have to walk the walk, *and* there will be days when it's going to hurt like hell. Sometimes it takes losing your mind in order to find your soul; but, there is a major upside to all of this. We attract *exactly* who we are to ourselves. With that equation, how can we lose? When you come together with another person who's consciously expanding their heart, mind and soul, deliberately self-actualizing, the energy fueling that type of relationship is indescribable. It's pure magic and much different than anything you may have experienced prior to your own metamorphosis.

Time gave me the gift of realizing I wasn't my parents, my friends or anyone else, but myself. This is *my* feature film. *My* love song. The fear of having the same experience as another person's horrible relationship or re-living a bad break-up went right out the window.

I've found what I'd always wanted and it was a wonderful relationship with me. And that, I believe, is the best place to start a quality relationship of any kind with another person.

Here's what I now know about making the "Dating Game" work in your best interest: Take the time to explore and enjoy your life, alone. Pray and meditate.

Figure your shit out, however painful it is. On the other side of that pain is a rainbow with YOU under it, living in the land of unimaginable possibilities.

When you think about it, what are six or twelve months in the course of a lifetime? (To get your act together and engage in a new, healthy relationship with yourself.) *It's a blink of an eye.* Remember: we are setting the stage for the rest of our lives!

Settling in our relationships—be it with a partner, the person we chose to be the mother or father of our children, even our friends—is not a viable option. Our time is too precious to waste on the wrong relationship, just because we're lonely. Blast through that lonely feeling! It's not real. *We are never alone.*

The main point is this: make sure your antennae are always up to detect whether or not you're settling for less—and as long as you're striving to embody the love you wish to experience, you'll never have to.

ENLIGHTENMENT IS SEXY CHAPTER TOOLBOX

Love Is In The Air

Spend time alone and focus on yourself—your desires, dreams and sense of purpose, your needs and wants, your beliefs and values.

Choose a spiritual practice and stick with it.

Don't settle, EVER.

4 Follow the Signs—Your Soul Already Knows

"Don't try to comprehend with your mind.
Your minds are very limited.
Use your intuition."

—Madeleine L'Engle

Last year, I conducted a wild experiment. For one month, I followed my gut instincts in every decision I made. No questions asked. That is, I lived intuitively, as completely as possible. Many people thought I was crazy, which is a testament to the way our society places logic so far ahead of intuition. However, my dabbling with what I consider to be "divine intervention" (i.e., my gut instincts equal God's guidance system for me) is ultimately what brought me here . . . writing to you.

Because of the many good results and successes I enjoyed during my month-long experiment, it quickly turned into a lifestyle, which I've now been living according to ever since. Humbly, I offer you a few "life lessons" I've gathered along the way.

- Follow the Signs.
- Embrace the Mystery.
- Trust the Universe.

1. Follow the Signs.

In his classic *Chronicles of Narnia*, C.S. Lewis writes,

> "But, first, remember, remember, remember the signs. Say them to yourself when you wake in the morning and when you lie down at night, and when you wake in the middle of the night. And whatever strange things may happen to you, let nothing turn your mind from following the signs."

When I initially began journeying upon this new path (of following my gut instincts, *no matter what*), one of the first things I noticed were "signs" that popped up like wildflowers, just begging for me to see their beauty or power. For example, one morning, I was in L.A. with my then-boyfriend, and we got a call from a friend who said he was with a big group of people (including two guys we knew) who were just about to drive out to an airfield two hours away in Santa Barbara and go skydiving -- and did we want to come? For me, I immediately saw it as a sign. I thought, *I don't care if it's a long drive! This is an opportunity to stretch myself, expand my boundaries, and know myself to be more limitless than ever.* I mean, I *felt* the universe calling out and saying, *Do this!*

"That is *so* cool," I said. "We have to go!"

Cutting to the chase, we all ended up having a totally kick-ass time skydiving, and I met a *bunch* of superb people in the process. But there was even *more* magic in store from my having chosen to "follow the signs" on this journey . . . because I *also* heard from one of the guys about a tiny little gourmet café that sounded phenomenal, even though it too was a long way away—about 1 ½ hrs. from the skydiving place.

When we finally got there and went in, we saw the place *was* really small—it had only 5 tables— and it was empty! Still, my intuition was telling me this was the right lunch-spot for us. It turned out that Bell Street Farm had been voted one of the top 100 restaurants in the country!

Five minutes after we sat down, Emilio Estevez and his mom came in and sat down right next to us. After hearing us sharing with each other about our morning's skydiving experience, he leaned in and said, "I'm a skydiver, too!" He started talking with us and we all became fast friends. By the end of the meal, he'd invited all of us to a Christmas party at his girlfriend Sonja's wine tasting room that night. Again, I sensed I should "follow the signs," so I decided to go. Instead of driving back, we booked a hotel and just hung out until the Christmas party. Once there, we were immediately welcomed by Emilio and Sonja and the rest of the group, as well. It felt like I was becoming part of this whole family comprised of a bunch of way cool people who lived in this small southern California town.

Was there more? Yowzah! It turned out quite a few of the people there were interested in what I was "into" and wanted to hear more about Transcendental Meditation. By the time I was ready to leave, Sonja invited me to come back to her wine tasting room and hold an event there to launch my company and talk about meditation.

Two months later, I was back at Casa Dumetz doing my first independent speaking gig. It was totally packed and people were lining up outside, doing all they could to either get inside or just stand there and listen in! I mean, *this was my first gig!* All this from rolling with my intuition and following the signs.

In other words, the Universe seems to have a knack for giving us direction and guidance, leading us forward from where we are to places, people or situations that are even better than any of us could imagine! All you have to do is pay attention to your intuition and be on the alert for anything that might be there to lead you to "something better" than your current experience. Obviously, I'd be irresponsible to NOT encourage you to "practice, practice, practice" tuning in and listening for (or watching for) those signs. Remember, practice makes progress. You *will* get better.

Another "sign from the Universe" to be watching out for is the kind that are there letting you know you're "on the right track," confirming for you or reassuring you that what you're doing or the direction you're heading is a good one. During spring break one year, while I was on a study abroad program in Greece, my friend Ben and I decided we would go to Italy for three weeks. Even though we were poor college students, we made it work by hitching a ride on an old ship packed with people that was setting sail for Bari. The point is, you can "follow the signs" even when all you have is a bottle of cheap wine and two tuna-fish sandwiches!

You just decide, "I'm doing this!" and don't worry about the how. I remember saying, "Who needs food, when we have a suitcase full of adventures?!"

We decided we would travel to Rome, Florence and Venice. When we arrived in Rome, it was Good Friday. We immediately went to the Vatican. I had to see it. When we got there, we walked around the square for a while and then realized that mass was starting in 30 minutes. We ran into the church and, to my surprise, there was hardly anyone there. I thought, *How is this possible?* We took a seat behind all the bishops and within fifteen minutes, mass started. Who would guess that Pope John Paul was sitting *just 15 feet in front of me?! HOW IS THIS HAPPENING?* When I turned around to look behind me, I saw hundreds and hundreds of people. I could not figure out how we got to sit so close to the altar! And remember, I was a Religious Studies major in college . . . and just a few pews away from the head of the Catholic Church! The words kept pouring through me, *This is an absolute miracle.* I was in awe, and felt so blessed, so cherished, so loved. I was in the presence of someone I considered a saint.

I immediately recognized how "following the signs" had led me here—I was getting another wave of fulfillment for earnestly pursuing my interest in comparative religions and not "hiding" what at times I'd "secretly" wanted: to openly and freely explore all dimensions of spirituality.

And speaking of "waves of fulfillment," there's an added "bonus" to following the Universe's signs: it's typically followed by a feeling of bliss, a jolt of happiness – like the Universe is rewarding you (like a dog) for listening! "Follow your intuition . . . follow your bliss!"

So, my suggestion is to use your power of observation to hone the skill of looking for and identifying the signs that show you the way to a better life. And as you do, allow yourself to marvel as the surprising connections and unexpected gifts roll in like the tide. Bestselling author Neale Donald Walsch says, "Built into you is an internal guidance system that shows you the way home. All you need to do is heed the voice."

When you follow the signs, you'll begin to feel like you're cruising effortlessly on autopilot . . . with a magical GPS system in tow. But be sure your seat belt is buckled! By more pro-actively tuning in to your intuition, relying more upon your inner guidance, and paying closer attention to (and following) the signs from the Universe, things *will* change! Very quickly, I found I'd embarked on a quest to literally see with my soul. I mean, I couldn't help it! I began seeing and feeling that *everything* is connected and nothing is a "coincidence." In fact, I was viewing the whole world through a new pair of glasses . . . and "the signs" began showing up everywhere!

This intuitively driven, signs-of-the-Universe-assisted "vision quest" inevitably led me (and I believe eventually leads us *all*) to a deeper connection to God and a clearer understanding of our life's purpose. With continued practice, you'll begin to see with your soul instead of your intellect. So-called "coincidence" turns into winks from the Universe, gentle nudges from the Divine and a sacred guide steering you in ever more fulfilling directions.

2. Embrace the Mystery.

If you decide you'd like to conduct an intuitive experiment of your own (similar to what I did), you'll probably want to eliminate the following phrases from your vocabulary:

"This shouldn't be happening."

"I can't do this."

"I have no idea who I am or where I'm headed."

"I have no direction in my life."

Why?

Because they attract to you what they are—negative, doubtful energy! Instead, choose to start saying the following things to yourself and others. And when you do, say them with a sincere sentiment of eager curiosity and heartfelt gratitude. Alright, now, repeat after me:

How did I get *here*?

Wow! Wowow!! Wowowow!!!

What cool-ass thing's going to happen *next*?!?

Prepare for life to get a *lot* more interesting and fulfilling.

Recently, an opportunity arose for me to "embrace the mystery" after I decided to celebrate New Year's a little differently than in past years. I wanted to be alone and in silence to really focus on what 2015 was going to mean for me. Mainly, I felt inspired to set the stage for a year filled with wonder and happiness. So, I headed to the mountains in Colorado to spend the start of the New Year at a Buddhist meditation center sitting on 600 acres high up in the Rockies.

Once I arrived, I wondered whether or not I would be lonely or sad, when everyone else I knew was partying and spending time with the people they love. However, what happened next was extraordinary. When the clock hit midnight, I felt a huge shift in my soul . . . like I had merged with the entire universe and could feel pure bliss running through my veins. The profound inner and outer silence I was experiencing seemed to lead me into direct connection with the Universe's great power . . . and being surrounded by magnificent giant statues of Buddha didn't hurt either! There was so much peace, both throughout my being and in the air, I felt utterly transformed. Now that's what I call a kick-ass New Year's Eve party!!!

Embracing the mystery of what is to come opens doors that one's mind deems crazy or impossible. However, I always seem to be "rewarded" for listening to my inner wisdom, not unlike a circus bear getting a treat every time he dances on two feet. Be open to what comes next, which requires you to let go of what you think "should" happen next. Practice moving with the flow of life—riding the Universe's wave—and with the understanding that as one door closes, it is a cue to move in a different direction.

3. Trust the Universe.

Steve Jobs, co-founder of Apple, Inc., once said, "You can't connect the dots looking forward; you can only connect them looking backwards. So you have to trust that the dots will somehow connect in your future. You have to trust in something—your gut, destiny, life, karma, whatever. This approach has never let me down, and it has made all the difference in my life."

As a child, I can remember sitting by myself and saying, "Be quiet and listen for the right answer." And, it always came. During those years, I never doubted that someone or some force greater than me guided my path.

Throughout my month-long experiment, I kept telling myself over and over, "Have no fear. You are protected. You are loved and you are guided. The signs will show you the way." It was my daily ritual, starting off each day having wacky conversations with myself. It didn't take long before I surrendered to the idea that the universe had my back always and completely. I came to believe in the infinite kindness of the Universe. I also found that having faith with a dash of courage is all that was required to make this "marriage" work.

Recently, I became transfixed on renting a house in the country to write this very book. I could not stop thinking about leaving the city and finding a quiet place in Iowa. Granted, when I slyly mentioned this idea to my friends, they thought I was crazy. Still, I had this gut feeling I would be able to write this book pretty easily, if I could just get myself some solitude. Without even trying, I stumbled on a cozy house, on 13 acres in the middle of the country . . . *exactly* like the one I had envisioned! I didn't even flinch. Sold! It was obviously meant to be.

Renting the house in the country changed my life significantly. It shifted my whole idea of how I wanted to live. I now know that I want to be surrounded by nature, live in a community of consciously evolving humans, and have access to the freshest food available to me. This represents a big switch for me, from living in a crowded city (Chicago's concrete jungle), eating out or getting take-out every night of the week and having a train run right next to my condo, to being in a small cozy house where I can see a night sky full of stars and hear the birds chirping while I drink my morning coffee. Yes, I have changed.

Alan Alda, the Emmy Award-winning actor, once said, "At times you have to leave the city of your comfort and go into the wilderness of your intuition. What you'll discover will be wonderful. What you'll discover is yourself."

With each day and each written page, I come to know myself—my *true* Self—a little better. Every day feels new and exciting and so full of promise. I feel totally alive and aware of the pulse of the earth beneath my feet. And that's really what I suppose I was wanting in the first place, when I set out to follow my instincts. In my mind, it's the *only* way to roll.

ENLIGHTENMENT IS SEXY CHAPTER TOOLBOX

Follow The Signs

(*This chapter has a toolkit
built into it—3 simple steps.)

Follow the signs.

Embrace the mystery.

Trust the Universe.

5

Everyone You Meet is a Mirror

"Love your enemies,
for they tell you your faults."

—Benjamin Franklin

When I graduated from junior high school, my mom wanted me to get a "broader education" than I'd gotten at the preppy, well-to-do school in suburban Chicago I'd just attended for three years. So, she decided to enroll me in this particular Catholic high school that drew in students from all over Chicago, inclusive of kids from every socioeconomic level, academic rank, race, religion and ethnic group.

Believe it or not, attending this Catholic high school helped open my mind. For the first time in my life, I was meeting kids who came from totally different backgrounds, which helped me to see *myself* more clearly. Differences in skin color, social standing, cultural backgrounds or religious beliefs did not separate me from my classmates. We were all teenagers excited about life. At my school, the kids I got to know were just interested in having fun and hanging out *harmoniously* with each other. I found it relatively simple to look past the differences between us and focus on our similarities, what united us. I *knew* we were all the same, and that's powerful stuff when you're in high school. Still, I didn't fully own it, and it took time for me to see this way consistently . . . *and* to go beyond that to an even more profound vision of people.

When I reflect on her decision to send me to a Catholic high school, I can see she did it because she wanted to make sure I stayed in line . . . but some core experiences I had there—specifically, the igniting of my senses about a "universal unity"—would actually serve me throughout my life. Even back then, I was learning my lessons about looking in the mirror.

But it wasn't always so easy. In high school, I used to throw the word "hate" around freely, as in: "I seriously hate that person." And yes, I'd say it half-joking. I mean, I didn't *really* hate that person. *Did I?* But yes, a piece of me was as serious about that hatred as a heart attack. Thoughts and feelings of hatred—as harsh as they seemed—seemed to come naturally to me. In a sense, hate was a part of me. Did I hate the way they looked—or the way they looked at me? Was it *them* I hated—or was it *me*?

I have come to realize it was me.

And this wasn't just something I "did" with people I knew from high school. Even after high school, I would meet someone and find myself immediately putting him or her in a category: "I like that person," "He's nice," "Oh, he's an asshole," "That girl is *smart*," "Her? She is dumb!" It literally never ended. In relationships with guys, I would accuse my boyfriends of being distant, inconsiderate or disrespectful; but in fact, I was just seeing myself. I was far from being mature and I was in fact the one who was being distant, inconsiderate and disrespectful. My relationships were just the Universe's way of showing me what I needed to work on. I was just too blind at the time to realize it, so I always accused my boyfriends of what were, in fact, my shortcomings.

For a long time, a deep-seated sense of helpless frustration held me hostage. My mom had cancer and I felt pissed. I was working night and day for someone else, which was a big source of frustration—I wanted to create something for myself (again, I come from an entire family of entrepreneurs). I felt trapped because I couldn't easily "fix" either of these situations. Consequently, simmering along with my frustration were feelings of resentment, anger and yes, hatred.

I *hated* that I felt helpless. I *hated* that I felt out of control. And, in turn, I hated others.

Life kept holding a mirror before my face, inviting me to see myself more clearly - the parts it'd be good for me to keep, the bits I needed to change, and the pieces I needed to set free. But, I stayed blind, busying myself so I wouldn't have to pay attention. The *last* thing I wanted was to face the dissatisfaction, the sadness, the helplessness . . . and the hatred I felt, which was actually reflecting back at me. It's so clear to me *now* the people I was meeting back then were revealing the worst parts of them . . . *ahem, I mean* me.

Ultimately, my mom ended up dying and the restaurant where I'd been working was sold to a bank. Since then, I've had ample opportunity to examine just how much good I did by focusing on *her* life and *someone else's* business and not choosing to create my own. In hindsight, I've realized that constantly focusing on everyone around you and not taking care of your *own* needs isn't the best route to take. I mean, I would have given my life to save my mom's, but it wouldn't have hurt to *simultaneously* keep balance in my own life and not completely lose myself in the process.

You might want to ask yourself, "Does that ring a bell?"

Eventually, as I claimed more responsibility for the contents of my life and started to open my eyes to the gifts I intuitively *knew* I needed to embrace, I began discovering *everyone* we meet is actually a divine mirror, offering us an opportunity to see ourselves with increasing clarity. After learning to meditate, I started literally seeing how we all *do* relate with each other on a more universal level . . . began actually seeing the divine threads that weave all of life together:

you
me
us
them
the birds
the trees
every living thing.

As I continued awakening to the wellspring of abundant love within and around me, the resentment, hate and hostility that had plagued me for so long began to diminish . . . and then fall to the wayside. Sincerely, I now can't remember the last time I used the word "hate" (let alone felt it). What seems to have replaced "hate" is this: deep, honest and fearless . . . love.

In the off chance I stumble across someone who strikes a nerve inside of me, I no longer think, "What a *loser* . . . God, I hate her." Instead, I turn inward and ask myself, *What can I learn from this soul standing before me?* I seek the gift. I listen for the lesson. I look to grow. And, I simply choose to send that person love. I offer up a prayer that they too might soon see the stroke of the divine underlying all things.

ENLIGHTENMENT IS SEXY CHAPTER TOOLBOX

Everyone You Meet Is A Mirror

When you recognize you dislike something in someone, know that it's really about you.

Once you identify your "issue," then take the opportunity (in that very moment, if possible) to focus on what this might mean for you.

Next, begin to work on letting go of that part of yourself that makes you irritated by others and replacing it with something more desirable.

6 Emotional Vampires

"Energy doesn't lie.
Keep sensing it, trusting it,
letting it liberate you."

—*Judith Orloff*

Whether we recognize it or not, we are all empaths[2] who are affected, to one degree or another, by the energy of those around us. When you step into a concert venue, the energy feels palpably different than it does at a funeral (one would hope). Generally speaking, the people with whom we interact, as well as those who surround us: a) fuel us, helping us to feel more alive and uplifted; b) drain us, leaving us to feel depleted and exhausted; or c) have little, if any, effect, due to their giving virtually nothing, nor taking anything away.

When was the last time you found yourself in a situation with someone who seemed to make you feel downright uncomfortable, or even suck the life right out of you? Maybe it was at a dinner party or when you were talking with a colleague in your office. Regardless of their background or status in life, the results are the same. After spending any length of time at all with these types of people, you feel energetically drained and often at least a little confused.

We ask ourselves, "Why do I feel this way? What the hell is going on?"

I'll tell you what's going on: you have just come into contact with an "emotional vampire." They may not suck your blood, but they *will* steal your

---

2 Acutely attuned to the feelings of others, empaths can actually feel another's pain and often are able to assist in their healing. Empaths typically possess the ability to really "see" or "hear" the other person, thereby affording them greater understanding of others.

energy in the blink of an eye. As revolting as it may seem, that is how they navigate their lives—that is how they survive.

And don't think just being "on a spiritual path" automatically makes you immune from meeting up with these energy-drainers. All of us inevitably experience these sorts of people at *some* point. The good news, though, is that as you begin to identify your limits and become stronger about taking a stand for your needs and desires, you will intuitively know how to set boundaries for yourself. For some, this comes from *repeatedly* being in situations that don't work for you at all, and finally just saying, "No more!" You finally start making decisions independent of anyone else's judgment or so-called "help," and you just keep moving forward.

So, my first suggestion for dealing with emotional vampires is: *Begin paying attention to how you feel with people.* Notice how in the presence of *some,* you feel empty inside, like you can barely take a deep breath . . . while around *others,* you feel full of life and vitality. So, for example, after you've felt shitty being around John or Jane Doe enough times, hopefully you begin to come to the end of your rope with them. You just *cannot* be around him/her without feeling pain or being forced to engage in their drama. And yes, you seem unable to get out of doing the same thing with them over and over again . . . and yet you expect a different result! But he/she never changes, and neither does the result!

One day, the interior light bulb comes on and you realize you can't take it anymore. You start to create boundaries. Yes, boundaries can be learned . . . and implemented immediately. You don't have to delay, girls, and you don't have to explain yourself to anybody. If you don't feel good around them, you don't need any other reason!

Sure, some people will want to grow with you and some people won't. The ones who want to just hang out in the same space probably won't find themselves in step with you. And that's okay. We are all on a different path. My point is, don't hold yourself back for anyone or anything. One major reason for being on this planet is to evolve and grow, right? I've found that any distraction from that mission is just part of the learning process. So, if you find yourself in an unhealthy relationship, get out of it! It's time to set some boundaries for yourself and get on with expanding your freedom of expression, your joy, and your potential! If John or Jane aren't supportive of you and your growth, usher them directly out the door and wish them the best! You've got a magical life to live!

Eventually, you get really good at this and you keep motoring forward, no matter what. You become a ninja at raising your consciousness, regardless of what others are or aren't doing.

You will find yourself naturally tossing *What-will-people-think?* to the wayside—which really pisses off emotional vampires—and continue focusing, instead, on what you're most wanting or really interested in.

Since emotional vampires prefer to keep you at a certain level—*their* level or lower—catching the attention of an emotional vampire poses a problem, especially for the person who is moving up the spiritual ladder. It's another obstacle you'll need to learn to navigate your way around.

So, if you feel ill, scattered or not your best self when a certain someone is around, "Run, Forrest, run!!" Avoid any unnecessary interactions with such people, and choose to set a boundary by deleting that person from your cell-phone, e-mail and social media contacts list.

On the flip side, we all know people who, when they walk into a room, we feel an immediate increase in the good vibes. When you are with a person who makes you feel alive, smart, creative and beautiful, then you know you've found someone from "your tribe." *These* are the people you want to be around and spend time with. This simple observation can serve as a means for you to choose your friends wisely, as well as the people you allow to spend any time around you.

With practice, identifying and deciding who you *want* to spend time with will become second nature to you. Preserving your *best* self will be your priority, and you'll know no one is going to "suck your energy" or stand in your way.

We have all heard examples of people who have lost tons of weight. All of a sudden, their friends become jealous or try to sabotage their progress. It's the opposite of what you would expect to happen. But the fact is: *When you change and grow in consciousness, the people around you may not.* The analogy of journeying up a mountain comes to mind. As you continue hiking, moving up into higher elevations, some people just won't be able or willing to make the climb with you. It's as simple as that.

The point is, if the people who were once in your circle don't have your best interests at heart, well, as painful as it may be, it's time to get new friends. We all have a choice to make, every moment of every day: whether or not to surround ourselves with people who will nurture and celebrate our growth and expanding happiness. For me, settling for less is just no longer an option.

Sometimes, it's not so easy, because there's a challenge in bringing forward the strength to separate yourself from people you've "hung with," but who you now know are emotionally draining you or holding you back in some way. For me, I learned this lesson the hard way.

After I began practicing T.M., just as quickly as my depression and sleep deprivation disappeared, a new life appeared before me. As I stepped forward into the flow of that new life, all sorts of doors started opening. I wrote this book, began meeting all sorts of cool people, and started a blog I love. With 100% of my being, I began to live my best life.

Quickly, I noticed some changes in my relationships. The men who had once interested me simply no longer did. As I had diverted my attention into "different" (better, higher) directions, those guys seemed to just vanish from my radar. Then, something else occurred. Seemingly out of nowhere, I started having problems with old friends. Some of my "best friends" started to snap at me for no apparent reason. Their hostility caught me off-guard, and I couldn't understand why they would act in such a way. I mean, why in God's name wouldn't your friends want you to be leading an amazing life? At first, it didn't make sense, but not everything on this side of life always does.

As I kept listening to my gut, paying attention to how I felt with these girlfriends—who no longer seemed to support me or even like me—I kept coming up with the same impression. I would leave them after a dinner or casual encounter feeling completely spent and depressed. *Um, no thank you.* Eventually, I could see what was happening. Though I had changed, some of the people around me had not. The writing was on the wall. It was time to move forward.

I realized that, in a way, the rules by which I *had* (but no longer) lived my life had been holding me captive—telling me who I should be friends with, making me say 'yes' when I wanted to say 'no,' and compelling me to censor myself in order to keep everyone happy. For years, these self-made, but mostly unconscious rules had lived rent-free in my mind. But, now I was ready to evict them.

It was heartbreaking and hard, but after years of trying to "push" to keep these relationships intact, I realized in a number of cases it just wasn't working. I finally had to let these friends go. I'd decided I had to trust the Universe, even when I didn't always know "why" or "how" . . . and this was simply another challenge I had to face, living in alignment with my decision. It was a tough choice, but I had to do what was best for me.

I resolved to send love to these friends of mine, and then I released them. In doing so, their push-and-pull, up-and-down energy was no longer able to penetrate me. I started to feel differently, like I had been let out of prison.

When we begin paying attention to how we feel around the people in our lives, "signals" will often show up right in front of us. Sometimes, they'll be loud and clear, and other times, they're more subtle, less obvious. But if we're willing to look and listen, we can recognize the best path forward in an instant. And our following such a "signal" can make all the difference in the world!

As you master this art—of listening to the wisdom within and paying attention to the Universe's signals—life naturally begins to feel easier, less chaotic and tiring. The range of people you'll likely encounter will be different than in your past, more positive, "life-supporting" and uniquely suited to where you're at in your journey forward. What's *really* going on in everything from job interviews to dates will become clearer to you. "Yes, this person is good for my soul" . . . or, "Nope, this person sucks the passion right out of me and I feel like crap around them. Next!"

The truth is, girls like us do best when we trust our gut. We don't have to sit around and think about it for weeks and weeks. We just know. So, we've got to "go" with our knowing and do what's best for you!

Sometimes, however, we can't cut off contact completely from emotional vampires. Maybe it's a family member or a co-worker. You can't really dump your family . . . or maybe you *can*. It depends how intense the feeling is. When you come in contact with this sort of person who you're "connected" with and yet you feel so drained you can't even function, what do you do? CODE RED!!! It's time to make an important decision. How much pain will you endure until you snap? Again, do you want to keep fighting it . . . or just listen to the signs and act upon them? Ultimately, there is no point in continuing to keep company with someone who is not going to help you grow or make you feel loved. This may mean you stop initiating contact with or responding to them, *even if* they are a family member. And yes, it may be you *finally* choose to look for a new place to work (or transfer to another part of the company *away* from your emotional vampire co-worker).

Here are a few "basic tips" I've found useful when it comes to dealing with emotional vampires who are also family members or co-workers/bosses. In these cases, I believe you *need* to put in safeguards and filters to take good care of yourself.

- Don't tell them anything about your life, because they may eventually use it against you.
- Don't share your opinion on anything of consequence to you, so you avoid the potential for their drawing you into an emotionally draining argument.
- Relating to the last point, since they don't care or don't like what you think, if you *do* tell them what you think, it will tend to aggravate them and incite them to further their agenda with you.
- Keep any conversation simple—talk about stuff that doesn't matter, like the weather.
- Keep the time you spend around them to a minimum.

- Move far away, if you have no alternative.
- Start saying "No" (firmly, when necessary) to things you don't want to do.
- If the emotional vampire starts getting aggressive, wizard mind-trick them by changing the subject, real fast (and keep going back to the new topic—they'll eventually get the message and quit).
- The bottom line? Protect yourself at all costs.

I believe you'll get the best results from listening to your inner wisdom. Trust me, you *already* know everything you need to know.

One last note about "protection": that is, protecting yourself when you encounter energy suckers. You can't control everyone who crosses your path, but you *can* guard yourself from harm. I have a little ritual that helps me tremendously. If I have had a rough day due to my having had a run-in with an emotional vampire, I will take a bath with Epsom salts. I make my tub a beautiful sanctuary by lighting candles, filling the tub with warm water, pouring in a couple of cups of Epsom salt, adding some lavender oil and just relaxing for 20 minutes. *Ahh-hh-hh*, that helps *so-o-o-o* much!

Sometimes, while I'm sitting there in the tub, I meditate or just relax in silence. Whichever I choose, this ritual really seems to help after a day of psychic warfare. It's easy, it feels good, and it works. Outside of that suggestion, you just want to build up your inner strength in order to protect yourself. You can do this through any of a vast array of spiritual practices (I do Transcendental Meditation for 20 minutes twice daily, which revitalizes my inner life), a healthy diet, plenty of rest and regular exercise. Be solid and consistent about it, though, so you can sail around your world and actually *keep* all of your energy. It makes a huge difference!

I believe there are people who are put on this earth to help us. You know them when you see them. Just being around them helps you build your confidence. They believe in your dreams and love you unconditionally. These "earthly angels" can come in the form of friends, mates, family members and strangers, and just seem wired to support you and carry you higher. It will be effortless to be around them. You can look in their eyes and feel the connection.

You know who I mean, right? So, hear this message loud and clear: *You want to fill your world with these people and avoid the emotional vampires as much as humanly possible.*

Remember, you and only you are in control of what happens in your life. *You* get to choose how you want to live and who you will allow in your space. When you see your life becoming brighter because of your choices, it will become easier for you. The Universe always rewards you for listening. You can count on that.

ENLIGHTENMENT IS SEXY CHAPTER TOOLBOX

Emotional Vampires

When you feel bad over and over around someone, take that as a definite sign to get away from them.

You are not crazy. If you feel down around certain people they are not right for you.

You come first. Always do what is right for YOU.

Don't let old rules hold you captive.

Don't say YES when you mean NO.

Build up your inner strength through an improved health routine and spiritual practices.

7 Don't Fit In

"To be yourself in a
world that is constantly
trying to make you something
else is the greatest accomplishment."

—Ralph Waldo Emerson

By nature, I think, we follow the pack. At least it seems that way when I look around. All over the world, I see so many people who appear to feel safe and content *following the herd*. And it's understandable. When we follow someone else's tracks, we think we have a good idea of the end result. "Jane went this way and look at how successful *she* turned out to be."

Stepping *off* the charted path and going our own way, though, takes courage. At times, it can seem as though we're lost or not in control. But what *do* we actually control anyway? Not much. Outside forces make this world turn. And where's the control *you or I* have if every single person on the planet has their hands gripped tightly around some plan, desire or dream they yearn to make real? However, understanding how relatively powerless we are actually sets us free. The freedom that comes with letting go and releasing our need to control is like none other. We become free to be ourselves and live out our true purpose, which I do *not* think includes "fitting in."

After I started meditating and felt like a new person, I thought to myself, "Alright, life is pretty awesome now, I want to be a business owner. I'm going to open a bar." Since I had been in the business for 15 years, it seemed like the next logical thing for me to do. And there wasn't a complaint in the house. Everyone around me was thrilled with the idea of me opening a bar in the middle of the city.

However, not long afterwards, when my plans changed and I did a 180-degree turn, deciding instead to work for a non-profit foundation, make NO money and talk to people about meditation, well, that was a whole different story. It started with both friends and family saying, "You're doing *what?*" "Do you want to be poor your whole life?" "When are you going to get serious about your career?"

I'm not going to lie, it really made me confused and hurt my feelings that people thought I was some sort of drop-out. In my mind, I was doing high-level spiritual work. And just like when I decided to become a Religious Studies major in college, I couldn't think of anything more important to do than to help people become whole. Finally, I decided, "Screw it! I'm doing what I know is right!"

Choosing to "not fit in" turned out to be one of the most important decisions I've ever made, giving me a new life, a great sense of happiness and loads of self-respect. If I would have listened to everyone around me, I would be sitting in a bar right now serving people whiskey, instead of helping them find deep spiritual fulfillment. So, yeah, I went with my gut on this one. Thank God.

I often tell my clients to be defiant. I'm not saying we all need to completely rebel against society and become hippies living in the woods or in a commune, but a dash of that sure wouldn't hurt. I understand we all have responsibilities, need to work and do our parts to preserve some sense of order . . . but why should we be tortured while doing it? That's no fun, and why shouldn't we all be having fun? *Misery is a choice.* And, there is *always* a different choice. Of course, in most of us, there's fear associated with change . . . and changing how you live your life—doing something different than those around you—can be scary. But the gift to be gained with change is freedom. Sometimes, we have to walk through fire to get to the Promised Land.

Channel your inner rebel . . . at least a little bit. A little goes a long way, really. Rebellion *can* be a spiritual experience, one that opens your heart to possibilities and phenomena that your mind once deemed impossible. Rebellion draws us into a more intimate space with truth. Those "zany ideas" you dreamed up on a whim start to solidify and eventually become an integral part of you. What were once "dreams" can quickly morph into "reality."

What I've found is we live in a world that feeds us a variety of illusions and lies about what it means to be happy and successful and beautiful. How many times have you thought, *If I could just get that promotion and make a little more money, I'd be sitting pretty* or *When I lose a little more weight, then I'll feel better about myself* or *Finding the love of my life will make me happy* . . . Hm-m-m?

And then—it never fails—these things happen and we have a brief wave of joy or a flash of elation . . . and then we immediately create a whole *new* list of things we believe will make us happy!

As the saying goes, though, "Happiness is an *inside* job." Following society's rules at the expense of your heart's most deeply held dreams is like saying, "I'm going to let fear dictate my destiny." We need to get real with our truest desires. We need to clearly identify for ourselves—by tuning in and listening to our hearts and souls—just what it is we most want and how we most want to live, regardless of what others think or will say. And then, get on your horse and start riding!

My point is this: each one of us has a gift and a higher purpose. Rarely do you just "figure it out" with no effort. Your quest might torture you, confuse you or scare you, but it will always teach you. You WILL grow into your "higher self," if the desire is there, and if you don't succumb to trying to fit in with the crowd, your family, your mate, your friends, with anyone! Then and only then are you ready to hit the ground running.

It's the same lesson I've been preaching throughout this book. Walk through the fire, face your demons, dive down into your soul—*that* is where the gold is. And that fire, endless love, limitless and boundless life energy, is in all of us. No one is excluded. It is your job to say, "Whatever, dude . . .

I'm going for it. I'm going to find out who I am and what I'm on this planet for, no matter what it takes." It's been shown to all of us over and over. One person, one single person can change the world. Now that is power. That is beauty. That is sexy.

And by the way, it's become crystal clear to me that the "Don't fit in" mantra is especially appropriate for women (and *especially* young women). I mean, who says we have to weigh 100 pounds to be considered beautiful? Who says we have to have a degree from Harvard to be considered brilliant? There is nothing sexier than a woman who knows who she is and owns it. She doesn't care what other people think, because she is so deeply invested in what *she* thinks. Her "home base" is her own soul. She doesn't waste her time and energy worrying about what her friends, co-workers or family think she *should* be doing. She has her own agenda. Sure, she respects their opinions, but ultimately knows they have no bearing on who she is and who she is destined to become.

Any and all narrow ideas that use words like "should," "should never," "have to," "need to," "must" and the like, dis-empower us and keep us from seeing our own (and others') magnificence. Each one of us has a higher purpose, to weave into the tapestry of the world the unique gifts and talents we possess.

We will NEVER ... let me repeat myself ... NEVER live up to the expectations of society. There will *always* be a smarter, younger, thinner, cooler human around the corner. But the good news is that when we realize we are one with the universe/God - at once, perfect and imperfect - we no longer feel a need to worry about fitting in with *them*.

When we let go and let God, we rise above the false self. *Self-doubt* exits, stage left. Hello, *Magic*, entering stage right.

If you love to paint, by all means, *paint*. If you love to sing, be my guest, sing your heart out. Not everyone will experience the caliber of success of Picasso or Beyonce. . but I say, it doesn't matter! Follow your passion for the sheer joy of it. That's right! No expectations of fame or untold wealth . . . Do it because *it makes your heart sing*.

Hate your job? Get the hell out of there!

People might think you're crazy when you decide on a dime to move across the country or quit your job and go to art school, but who cares? *You are not here to fit in and follow the crowd!*

When you start following your bliss you never know what doors may open. Nothing cool is going to happen to you if you just sit in your cubicle all day and hate your life. Again, you may not turn into Jennifer Lopez, but you may meet the man of your dreams while you're singing your heart out on karaoke night (or run into a "random" person at an art class that has the PERFECT job for you.) See where I'm going with this? You have to walk down the corridor of life to have the magic doors open for you!

You're here to live your *own* life. Spread your wings and be who God created you to be - a blazing star! This world *needs* people who inspire the highest and best in us to come alive, who expand our awareness and make us think with fewer limitations, who help us love a little deeper. The people around you may believe you're nuts at first, but in the end you will inspire them to go for their dreams. You will stand out, without even trying, as a leader, a trailblazer, and a teacher.

"Don't fit in." What does that even mean? Stop trying to fit into someone else's idea of life! Stop trying to fit into some image of success at work or that pair of jeans! Be your own rule maker! Look for your own sense of perfection. Set the stage for your own truth to guide you . . . because at the end of the day, your happiness is all that matters.

There is a universal voice that speaks to all of us. You just have to be quiet enough to hear it. And when you do, it will guide you amazingly well and light your way with wonder.

ENLIGHTENMENT IS SEXY CHAPTER TOOLBOX

Don't Fit In

Follow your bliss. It's there for a reason.

Don't listen to people that don't get you anyway. They are just scared, so they're pushing their crap on you.

Have fun! Misery is a choice.

Don't let fear dictate your destiny.

Don't be a sheep.

8

Stop Being Married to the Results

"Act without expectation."

—*Lao Tzu*

We have all heard the advice: "Live in the present moment." Easier said than done. *Or is it?* When we stop chasing after a specific future we think we need . . . or running away from some vision of the past with which we want to avoid entanglement, we simply live *now*, and life opens up to us. We are in the flow of the world, which is where happiness lives. See, I think what so many wise men and women throughout history have said—in various ways—is true: *Everything is in God's time, not human time.* If you really think about it, we don't control much of anything outside of us—*especially* "time." What we *do* have control of is our own attitudes, beliefs and decisions, including our willingness to trust.

When we understand this and begin to trust in "something greater than ourselves," we start to disconnect from the end result. We leave that to God/the Universe/the Powers That Be/whatever you want to call it. One's fulfillment in the "doing," in the "being a part of" (the 'Dance of Life') becomes enough. Are you really *needing* to know how the story turns out, if you're in love with the words you're reading now?! When you naturally feel content with whatever is happening in real time, the results of your action aren't something you *need* to have turn out a certain way. In other words, you're not married (or attached) to the specifics of the results.

For example, when I was just about to graduate from high school and had been accepted to attend

Salve Regina University, a small, prestigious school in Rhode Island (where my older brother Peter had been a student), I eventually chose to follow my intuition and *not* go to college (at that time). Knowing how wild I could be in an environment like that, I decided instead to get an "adult" job in Chicago (working at the Mercantile Exchange) and roll with life from there. Mainly, I didn't feel it was necessary to be on the same timeline as everyone else ("You just graduated from high school? Oh, you *need* to go to college right away!"), nor did I want to allow the world to dictate to me. I thought, *I'd rather exercise my freedom to go forward on my own path, thank you very much, even if I'm not sure how it'll turn out.*

I came out with a cool job, a totally different experience than everyone else and, above all, stayed true to what I wanted to do. (By the way, I ended up starting off making $600 a week and living in an apartment in Lincoln Park, an oasis for young professionals and students . . . right out of high school!)

But "acting without being married to the results" can be hard, given all the rules society can throw your way. People like Steve Jobs, Maya Angelou and Richard Branson have attributed their successes largely to following their inner prompts and not worrying about the results, regardless of how many naysayers they faced.

The fact is, everyone has the choice to say "yes" to tuning into and following their inner guidance. Interestingly enough, when we *are* holding hands with the Universe, we're much more likely to be happy, just by virtue of that connection—not because we "got" or "achieved" this or that from the outside. The simple act of being connected to the wellspring of life brings us palpable joy. We no longer yearn and ache for material things or status or relationships to fulfill us. In this state, we forget what being unhappy feels like. On top of it, when we are simply living in and for the present moment, everything unfolds in a more organic fashion, devoid of our self-imposed pressures and expectations, thereby allowing what's *real* to come forward and really shine.

Be aware, though, the ego doesn't like when you're not fueling it, when it doesn't have its normal control over you, when you're not catering to the "image" it compels you to exude. Indeed, your ego is the primary proponent of your subscribing to a false reality. And both our egos and the collective consciousness around us do not take kindly to free thinkers. People who question the "system." The ego is best friends with "the world that has been pulled over your eyes to blind you from the truth" (*The Matrix*). And to go beyond that belief system, at first, puts you into hot water with the social constructs around you. First you feel pain, then confusion, then some anger, because everything around you seems to tell you that you're wrong, crazy or totally delusional. However, that is just your ego digging its claws in you.

It's important to remember: *Your thoughts are not "who you are"—they're whatever you're choosing to put your attention on for the moment.* A lifetime of "being rational" and following the rules you are taught -- where has that gotten you? Right NOW is the time to let go of any tendency you might have to dwell in the past or the future. Focusing your attention on "future results that need to occur for me to be happy" means you're focusing on your intellect. I believe we would actually lead freer, healthier, more joyful lives if we'd focus less on the rational mind, and more on our intuitive knowing and our "higher" consciousness—the realities found when one is living in the present moment. Practice using your intuition to guide you in your decision-making, even in the small stuff. Seek to be fully alive in the present moment. When you are in this state, your soul will provide you with whatever guidance and deep understanding you need. *Everything that is good lives in the now.*

In other words, don't always do things for a result. When doors open, walk through them. Trust in a higher power. Have an empty mind, and allow the Universe to fill it with all of the magic that is infinitely available in the world. Ultimately, that means just *being.* Taking it all in and, above all, taking it as it comes. Use faith to bolster you along the way, if you like. Sure, it may be a bit difficult at first, but if you just surrender to this idea of "don't be attached to the results," life will become much sweeter.

You know, my learning to meditate was something I did because a door opened in front of me—I had no real clue at all about what the "results" would be (although people who seemed to know what they were talking about *and* cared about me had told me "positive" benefits could be expected). Ultimately, I had an "awakening" with my first meditation, and yes, the "results" have generally been *way* good ever since.

At every moment of the day, the Universe is feeding us inside information, showing us the way. We need to be listening and watching for these "signs." (Obviously, I had to be paying attention to the Universe's signals for me to learn TM, in the first place.) In this regard, it's so important to live for *right now* and not yesterday or tomorrow. The consequences of ignoring what's showing up for us *here and now* are not good. They lead to anxiety, depression and a boatload of hopelessness—worrying about the future and regretting the past. When we surrender to a Higher Power (by whatever name), it is so much easier to live. Become in accord with the Universe--we all have a destiny, accept it. Don't refuse to accept things that happen to you. It is all part of a "bigger plan" . . . a "divine plan." There is a reason for everything. Stop asking, "Why is this happening to me?" and start saying, "Uh-oh, I must be getting off track!" You are being guided down your path. Sometimes you can't see it until you look backwards, but there is a purpose. So stop looking at your experiences as good or bad. That is your ego speaking. It's you letting your emotions get the best of you. If you can rise above that, life will become so much easier. There is intelligence behind all of this. It's the reason everything works in nature, why you are born perfect, and why at the end of your life you can look backward and connect the dots.

As I always say, "Roll with it." The only thing you have control over is your perspective. You *can* choose to live a kick-ass life. All it takes is a willingness to accept the things you cannot control and the readiness to surrender… AND GO FOR WHATEVER.

Accepting things as they are also helps keep you calm. And the irony is that when you take on a "detached from the results" attitude, you often end up being so calm, you actually become *more* effective and productive in your life, and have a *better* and *deeper* impact on the world. Eventually, I believe this approach leads to "higher purpose" living.

I wake up every day and have a mental conversation with God. I always say, "Thank you for giving me enough brains and freedom in my soul to allow You to work through me." I know God's dream is way bigger than mine, and I've realized I can't be bothered with trying to figure all this out. There is *no way* I will be able to . . . and I know it! So I simply stopped trying. That cut my problems down *big-time* and totally elevated my happiness. I stopped trying to be my own psychiatrist, and simply said, "Alrighty then! You take the reins." And thankfully, God listened.

When you find what you love to do, the act itself makes you happy, accomplished and truly alive. You can and will be detached from feeling the need for specific results. Funnily enough, this approach to life almost always leads to some sort of success. In other words, when you choose to force nothing, you'll likely find that everything flows to you.

I believe to just be happy to be alive is the ultimate spiritual secret. No past, no future, just now. Learn to live this way and the results will be like sweet and fabulous icing on the cake of your life.

ENLIGHTENMENT IS SEXY CHAPTER TOOLBOX

Stop Being Married To The Results

When you love what you do,
the joy in the work is enough.

Take life as it comes.

Live in the NOW.

9

Write it Down and Make it Your Reality

"Throw your dreams into space like a kite, and you do not know what it will bring back: a new life, a new friend, a new love, a new country."

—*Anais Nin*

Whether you believe it or not, you have the ability to increase the likelihood that your dreams become a reality. I know this for a fact. I have personally experienced it many times. The "how" is simple. I will sit down and write exactly what I want to happen, in detail, and then forget about it. Time goes by and one day, I inevitably will find myself stumbling upon a "wish list" I made or a couple of lines about something my soul wanted, *which I'd put down in writing*. You can imagine the shock on my face the first time this happened, when I realized that *precisely* what I'd earlier asked for—and wrote about—had actually happened in my life!

And yes, that "first time" was a long time ago. Looking back, the strange part is that I always, *always* forget that I'd written down my desires. However, not long ago, I started to really take note of these frequent occurrences, asking myself questions like, *How do these little miracles arise? Can I look backwards, trace my steps, and find out "the key" to what makes these happen?*

After a fair amount of persistent observation, I *did* uncover the mystery . . . and what I discovered was simple, but truly mind-blowing. I realized I was *writing letters to the Universe* . . . and like a cosmic game of tennis, the Universe volleyed them back to me as my new reality. This was a fantastic game that I wanted to be playing *more consciously*, making the Cosmos my partner.

Let's look a little more closely at this phenomenon. For me, it always starts off the same way. I will have a thought that forms into a desire. In the case of this book, I first just had this faint thought to write a book. It started years ago, but I had no idea why I kept thinking it . . . this perpetually recurring thought that I should put my very best down into the pages of a book. As the years went on and my life started to change, I randomly started blogging. When people began connecting to my words, I saw that as a "sign" and wasted no time: I decided the thought floating in the back of my mind for all those years was now ready to become my reality. In fact, it was clear to me that original thought had morphed into a deep desire to write a book.

And it occurred to me that instead of banging my head against the wall, I would just ask the Universe to help me write it (i.e., I would not "try" to make—or force—anything to come out a certain way.) I started by making a list of topics I would like to write about. Then, I wrote out a list of who I wanted to design the cover, who would design the interior of the book, who would be my publicist, who would help me launch the book, what date I would release it, and on and on. I wrote out every single detail about this book and its future.

Writing out every last detail did a couple of things for me. First, it was a complete mental dump. Any fear I had seemed to dissipate, as all the details were now worked out on paper. I released all the anxiety about the "unknown" from my mind and as a result, I was clear as a bell. Second, it gave this "project" a sense of order. Once my desire was fully stated and down on paper, I was able to tweak it, make sense of it and organize it. *Wow!* I thought, *I'm actually going to do this.*

The book started to take shape and become alive. Third and most importantly, things began to happen, seemingly out of nowhere. That kick-ass publicist I wanted to work with? I knew someone who told him about me, and he eventually said he would love to work with me. The topics I wanted to write about? It became perfectly clear how I was going to write about them. The words seemed to just flow out of me. Information seemed to just drop into me out of nowhere. *This book was writing itself.* Did I want a top-shelf editor? One contacted me after reading a blog-post I'd written. . . and he (Willy Mathes) turned out to be the most amazing editor I could have ever found. Soon, *he* referred me to George Foster, who designed this book's killer cover design! (Did I say both were also long-time meditators and super-cool to work with?)

I only realized *months later* (after I found the list I'd made) that all of this was unfolding *exactly* as I'd written it down. Wowza! Someone or something *somewhere* was listening to me!

A lot of motivational speakers and business experts talk about writing down your goals to increase your productivity. And it's true: clarifying your thoughts and goals *does* make you more productive. Of course, this is a really positive result you can get in your work life. What really fascinates me, though, is the fact that this "formula" works for relationships, too! And health and any other area of life you're interested in improving or creating. You say you want to get into a good relationship? Write down *exactly* what you are looking for. Down to the very last detail. The Universe is listening, but you need to be *very* clear about what you want.

Now comes the subtle, not so obvious part. *You better be seriously ready for what is coming.* Once you put your deep desires and dreams out there, the Universe starts working on making them happen. Yes, you have taken the necessary steps to put the wheels in motion *and there is no stopping that train.* My next suggestion? *Start living as if you have already received what you are desiring.* If it is a wonderful love partner you're looking for, start talking to him or her. Tell them, "I am ready for you to come into my life." Then hold on to your hat, because they are coming. I tell my clients, start getting your life in order so when your wishes are fulfilled, you're ready to roll with them. Pay off your debt, get your apartment in order, get rid of clutter, get healthy--just get your shit in order. You are showing the world, here I am and I am ready. Bring it!!

I also like to put the date on my desires as I write them out. Then, when they come true, I date them again. I keep a gratitude journal, in which I'm able to give thanks for specific things I've received, and I can actually see how truly the Universe is supporting me. As my heart's desires become my reality, I have an actual date telling me when it happened. This "evidence" is empowering. (I feel it's super powerful, really!) Not that any of us need proof, but it's fun *and* makes my faith in this "cosmic partnership" even stronger.

It actually blows my mind every time I go back to my list of desires and realize that everything seems to happen almost without any effort on my part. I write it down and let it go. What happens after that is none of my business. I doubt I'd ever be able to figure out all the strategies required to "make" this or that happen anyway, so why bother?

Once you know the Universe is really listening to you and how much support is really out there for you desires and dreams, everything changes. You don't have to be so hard on yourself. You don't have to obsess about timelines. You know there are no boundaries on your mind—that is, you're free to think as big or as small as you please. But remember: this world isn't here so you can play *small*. If it makes you feel better, you can start with small requests, but soon enough you'll be asking for more and more, and bigger and better "assistance" from the Universe. You will KNOW that everything in this world is, indeed, a gift from the Universe . . . and *that* makes for a super-exciting life.

There is one catch to all of this. You can never use this plan to bring harm to anyone. In other words, you can't say, "I want my manager to get fired, so I won't have to put up with her crap." It will blow up in your face. Know that the Universe has enough for all of us. Enough love, money and support—whatever you need, it's got. You don't need to take from others or wish harm on anyone. There are laws set in place to take care of other people's bad behavior. Trust me. And once again, that is not your job. I can't stress that enough. I always have to remind people that when you're manifesting, the purity of the desire is very important. Even wishing your enemies love is a good practice. It allows you to release and resentment in your soul and make room for the good stuff.

So, get your "Carpe Diem" notebooks out and start writing away. Describe all your deepest desires and dreams in detail. Talk to the Universe . . . It's paying attention to you. It wants you to be lit up, and to really *live*!

ENLIGHTENMENT IS SEXY CHAPTER TOOLBOX

Write It Down and Make It Your Reality

Write down what you want, *in detail.*

Get ready, because it's coming. Get your shit in order, because all your dreams are very likely going to come true.

Date the page when you write out your wishes, and then date them again when they come true.

Keep a gratitude journal, thanking the Universe for all of its awesome gifts!

10 Stepping Into Your Dreams

"She believed she could, so she did."

—R.S. Grey

Dreams, we all have them. The difference is: some of us will live them and some of us won't. I used to think it was easy to accomplish whatever you wanted. *What's the big deal!* I thought. I'd walk into a store and think, *This person wanted to open a store and they just did it.* Boy, was I wrong! I've discovered it typically takes some mega-sized cajones and serious perseverance to accomplish your dreams.

I mean, a new reality doesn't just fall out of the sky and into your lap. It takes clear vision, planning, persistence, and a commitment to taking the right action, day after day, no matter what. I know in many spiritual circles the mantra is: "Do less and accomplish more." I get how that fits in, but sometimes we just need to hold the dream in front of us, roll up our sleeves and throw ourselves headlong into action.

If you talk to people who have gone out there and kicked some serious ass—in terms of achieving a big dream—you will find the vast majority of them saying that every step of the way, their diligent efforts and one-pointed focus were part of the process—in fact, were alive and well on a daily basis.

Sure, there may be moments when you'll question your sanity, cry like a baby and feel like you're at the end of your rope. No one, and I mean *no one*, gets ahead in life without massive action. To sit back and just wait for life to come to you is not how this party is going to get started.

See, the reality is you'll very likely require a little or a lot of both of these approaches, as you move in the direction of fulfilling any dream. Without a shadow of a doubt, though, first you'll need to get "the inside" right. What I mean is this: *connecting to something greater than yourself on a daily basis is at the core of the dream process.* As we all oughta' know by now, *that* is where the magic happens, from the inside out. The juice comes from connecting to the Universe, connecting to your "sacred" self. *Then* you're ready to turn into Action Jackson.

Most of us have learned that the best way to connect to a "Higher Power" is either through meditation, prayer or some sort of spiritual practice. Regularly engaging in some technique or daily routine in our lives will help take us beyond our mind and connect us to the Universe/Spirit/God, the source of support for anything good (e.g., your dream) manifesting.

Second, we need to get crystal clear on what we want . . . really digging deep to reveal what we want to do with our lives. In my case, ever since I can remember, I have been fascinated with spirituality, religion, psychology and humans, in general. I used to fantasize about being a motivational speaker with a spiritual angle. The problem was, I never thought in a million years I would be qualified for the job. Talking about spirituality was meant for older men with white hair who were a hell of a lot wiser than I was.

In time—it's taken me many years—and through experiencing some major ah-ha moments, dealing with loss and doing some serious soul-searching, I've gotten to where I'm at, which is not precisely the dream I originally had, but a variation that feels aligned with who I feel I am today: an awakened woman who travels the world, writing books and blogs, and coaching anyone who wants help with their own awakening and empowered emergence. That is the dream I'm living today . . . and hot damn, it *is* fulfilling!

I'm not saying accomplishing *your* dream will be easy, but I highly doubt it will be off-the-chain impossible, either. Once you're regularly connecting to your Higher Power and living your "dharma" (life in accord with universal laws), there will be a natural flow to your efforts and greater support for their fulfillment. Yes, often enough you will be working your ass off, but it won't be torture . . . *because you are doing what you want.*

The point is, with a one-two punch of a well-connected inner life and a focused, pro-active outer life, you'll be much more likely to see your dreams come true.

And really, I never thought in a million years I would be in the position I'm in now. I feel like finally, after years of frustration, I am doing *exactly* what I always wanted to do. Why wasn't I able to figure this out earlier? I'll tell you why: I wasn't ready. I think the Universe has a special time clock and when it's your time, that's when the fun starts. I started seeing the signs leading me to my destiny, and I made the bold choice to say, "Okay, I'm going for it!" Whether it was getting the job working with Oprah's team or being invited to speak about meditation, I see now they were all signs. And finally I thought, *My dream actually has legs. I'm going to go whole-hog and give it my all. If it doesn't work out, I still will come out on top, because I am devoid of any regrets.*

Now, let's talk about some of the hurdles you may face as a dream-seeker:

1. When you start really living your truth and going towards your wildest dreams, some of your clos-est peeps often start acting wonky with you. You will be a constant reminder of *their* dreams—you know the ones they never pursued (for reasons a, b & c). When your partner, family or friends start acting bonkers around you, or try to stop you for going for it, remember: it's not you, it's them. Just keep moving.

2. Really going for a dream takes a lot of personal commitment and, well-… letting go of things. To clear the path for your future dream to be a reality—to successfully launch a new business or attain a credential you've needed to "get to the next level" in your field (or to achieve any such

dream)—you'll have to get rid of as many distractions as humanly possible. Setting your sites on your goals can often swallow up a lot of your time . . . and since there are only 24 hours in a day, you're going to have to make some room. If you really want to make things happen, dreamwise, you'll need to prioritize. What is more important to you: going out for dinner with your friends 3 nights a week or staying in to work on your kick-ass business plan? Do you want to spend 100's of dollars on new outfits every week or do you want to start saving for a fabulous new website to sell your products? You get the idea: prioritize your dream now and celebrate later!

3. Heads up, all you dream-weavers! You just might need to make one or more radical changes in your life. Do you want to be a movie actress, but you live in Tulsa, Oklahoma? Time to start thinking about how you're going to move yourself out to Hollywood or NYC! We read about it all the time: child actor has a dream and family responds by moving everyone out to California to give her/him a shot at making it in the big leagues. I've heard all sorts of wild stories: people living in trailers, eating nothing but Ramen noodles, because they are dirt-poor . . . but still never giving up. The determination of a mother, the perspective of an eagle and the strength of an elephant? Yeah, sometimes, that's precisely what it takes.

4. Vagueness or lack of clarity on any level can turn a great dream into a nightmare. Having a clear idea (or at least a pretty darn good idea) where you're going is vital to living your dreams. Anyone can lie in bed and imagine what their "ideal life" would look like . . . but without putting the pedal to the metal, those visions ain't happening anytime soon! What to do? Write it all down! Yep, planning, planning and more planning! The cool part about coming up with a solid plan is that you can break your dream manifestation down into sections. That way it doesn't feel overwhelming to you. But I'm careful to leave room for the Universe to give me guidance about "The Plan." (That is, I do whatever I can to navigate the flow between my plan and God's plan.) I always say, "I'm waking up in the morning, checking my daily plan, and just putting one foot in front of the other."

5. Losing sight of the importance of balance. When I'm "runnin' down a dream" (as Tom Petty would say), I need to keep tabs on how well I'm combining my spiritual life with my day-to-day life. When we regularly meditate or do yoga or walk in nature, we stay more connected to the Universe. That is where your major ideas or minor adjustments will come from . . . your direction in life, your million-dollar ideas or your valuable little tips. The more tapped in you are,

the smoother your journey will be. But a balanced life—eating well, getting enough sleep, avoiding overly stressful or toxic situations and people, etc.—is also part of the "healthy balance" required to successfully achieve a dream.

Most of us are going to have to bust some monkey-ass along the way to get to the top of our mountain . . . but proactively gathering support from every imaginable front, we can handle most any obstacle without breaking a sweat.

Hopefully, by this time, we understand that challenges or setbacks in life actually offer us an opportunity to grow and learn. When we have major life goals, we'll be wise if set them in place and ready ourselves for some major learning spurts. From what I've seen, if you really move towards your best life, you're going to grow so much you won't even recognize yourself when you accomplish your dreams. What you're passionate about *is* your true destiny. I believe such dreams are placed in your soul before you even landed on this earth. They're what you set out to do . . . and damn it, you should give 'em your all, no matter what. Trust yourself and your dreams, take action and stay on your intention, seek guidance from the Universe, meet each challenge with patience and a clear mind, and you *will* be shown a way forward.

Yep, I know one thing for sure: you'll get a feeling of peace and joy in chasing your dreams and living your truth with which nothing else compares.

ENLIGHTENMENT IS SEXY CHAPTER TOOLBOX

Stepping Into Your Dreams

Get *crystal clear* on what you want.

Take massive action.

Make sure you are connecting to the Universe on a daily basis (or moment-to-moment, if necessary).

11

The Underestimated Power of Simplicity

"Life is really simple, but we insist on making it complicated."

—*Confucius*

When I decided I really wanted to change my life and move forward at rocket speed, I decided to take an inventory of my life. At first, I started small. I thought to myself, *I'll clean out my closets and see how I feel.* I put on an awesome music playlist, cleared off my dining room table and started making piles. As I pulled dress after dress out of the packed racks of clothes, I thought to myself, *Who the hell bought all these clothes?* It almost seemed like I was looking at someone else's wardrobe—as though an entirely different person had stocked my closet! *I would NEVER wear that.* Then, I would simply add it to the "Absolutely not" pile.

As I continued to remove items that were *never* going to be on my body again, I noticed I wasn't playing the lying game with myself. You know the one: "I haven't worn these pants in 5 years, but I'll wear them someday." Or the one I love the most: "This dress is 3 sizes too small on me, but after I do my juice cleanse, it will totally fit me." In other words, as I purged my closet, I also eliminated the bullshit.

This method differed from how I *used* to organize my stuff. My old pattern was to let things get so out of control I would freak out even thinking about my disorganized life. This time around, I was going to tackle and eliminate *anything* that stood in my way. I wanted peace and order. Yes, I was on a mission from my higher self.

I then decided to have my friends over and give them anything they wanted from the "over-it" pile. This little act started me on an epic clearing trip. With every purse that went out the door, my spirit became a little lighter. I was digging this feeling. To me, it felt like freedom.

I decided I would go through every drawer, every cabinet, every piece of mail and all of my books, and give away anything I no longer needed. I gave myself one medium size box dedicated to memories: old letters, concert tickets and pieces of my past I wanted to keep forever. Other than that, if I didn't need it, it went out the door. By the time I got finished, I had 12 boxes for the Salvation Army *and* I felt like I had released the energy of 5 crazy people from my body—much lighter and totally clear. And dig it! My space was now simple, clean and clutter-free!

It was obvious to me how simplicity helped fuel my soul in my home, so I decided to carry it into every part of my life.

My finances seemed like the next logical step in this process. I swear on my life I cannot see numbers. I have always been awful with math. My palms start sweating when tax season arrives, and in the past, I always made my bills way more complicated than they needed to be. I just didn't want to deal with it.

Times had changed, though. I wanted a whole lot more control of where my money was going every month. I spent a lot of time going over each and every bill. Getting rates lowered and cancelling things like cable and magazine subscriptions I wasn't really getting true satisfaction from anyhow. Things I'd grown to feel were total time-wasters and space-eaters.

I also came up with a plan to pay off any debt I had. I was looking for simplicity and not wanting to waste energy on paying back big banks. When all was said and done, I had cut down my bills in half. In 6 months, I paid off any debt I had and put what bills were re-occurring on auto-pay. *What in the world had I been thinking before?*

Because my math phobia had gotten the best of me, I was being drained by bills I should have never had in the first place. With some applied focus, diligent effort and a burst of some temporary hard work, I was financially free. Check that one off the lineup!

With regard to my friendships, I started making lists: Friends Who Make Me Feel Good and Friends Who Don't. I paid attention to my feelings when I was with different people, journaled about it, and made some decisions. I picked my battles. If an important event was coming up that I felt compelled to attend with various "emotional vampires," I would take extra time to care for myself before joining up with the group. Maybe I would meditate 10 minutes longer or have a healthy breakfast or even make sure I got enough sleep the night before. Little things to keep me centered. In other words, I now knew what I was committed to doing if I was going to walk into a tricky situation. And *only* if I felt it was really necessary.

Other than that, I stuck to my guns. Because of forces much bigger than myself, some people were just not healthy for me to be around. They didn't make my life easier—in fact, they complicated everything. I was out to live simply, and anything or anyone not fitting into that had to go. My list was made and I was sticking to it. The results? Day after day, I kept growing lighter.

On and on I went. Just really paying attention to this feeling I had inside every time I made my life a little easier. I went so far as to work with an amazing life coach for months to rid myself of old ideas and false beliefs that no longer worked with my new-found happiness. It was as though I had moved on to cleaning out my mind. The En Vogue song lyrics played repeatedly in my brain, "Free your mind and the rest will follow."

Piece by piece, I made room for new ideas and new people to come to me. So many little compli-cations had taken up shop in my mind, but with a one-pointed dedication to a simpler, better life, I evicted all of them. I soon found myself living in a drama-free zone. I finally got to the point where I truly felt I had created an "easy like Sunday morn-ing" existence. I had a clean slate from which to grow. And boy, did I grow.

At this point, I purposely only worked part-time. I could see the big picture and I wanted to have as much time as possible to write and plan out my future. My bills were half of what they'd previously been, so why not? I can remember waking up in the morning with an unbelievable feeling of peace. My house was in order, healthy food filled my fridge, time was on my side and all my worries had left my mind. I was ready to create.

Words started flowing out of me as I wrote this book. I had more time to spend with good friends who fueled my passions. My energy levels increased, and I was getting twice as much done is half the amount of time. I spent hours cooking healthy meals for myself and savoring every bite. I felt in tune with life. I knew I had made some really healthy decisions, and I felt I was being rewarded for them.

From this whole cleansing process, I realized what I had been doing before: ignoring my problems, letting the bills pile up, ignoring my instincts, and letting a chaotic life get the best of me. This was the *opposite* of simplicity and peace. This does not work, and it actually takes us further away from our true selves. Thankfully, I got the message, did what I needed to, and was set to receive the "good stuff" the Universe had in store for me!

The fact is, when you ask the Universe for something, get ready for the response, because it's coming. That is, get your house and relationships and mind in order. Be prepared to take responsibility for receiving what you're asking for: if you're requesting a "new and better relationship," do what's required (e.g., make sure you're not an emotional mess, your house isn't a rat-hole, etc.). Doing your part to ensure you'll be able to receive a healthy relationship, greater abundance or increased health just takes envisioning what's necessary for that picture to unfold in your life . . . and saying "yes" to just doing it!

When we start removing what no longer serves us, what remains is a world filled with love and positivity. We become free to create and to live out our dreams. The day-to-day grind becomes lighter, because it's that *grind* that steals your life energy from you. It would like to keep you on a metaphorical treadmill—constantly running in place, but never taking you anywhere.

No, happiness isn't about buying stuff you can't afford, hanging out with people who don't lift you higher, or saving every skirt that comes your way in hopes of "one day." The only day that is going to rock your world is "today." *Choose NOW to do what you can to make life simple.* Clear out the clutter in your home and in your mind. There is a genius trying to climb out. A knower of life. This sheer awesomeness is within all of us. It's just hard to get there when you're tripping over all your "stuff."

ENLIGHTENMENT IS SEXY CHAPTER TOOLBOX

The Underestimated Power of Simplicity

Clear your clutter.

Get rid of anything and everything
you don't need.

Introduce order to every area of your life.

12 Set Yourself Free With Forgiveness

"As I walked out the door toward the gate that would lead to my freedom, I knew if I didn't leave my bitterness and hatred behind, I'd still be in prison."

—*Nelson Mandela*

Since us enlightened girls want to play in the present, and hatred keeps you stuck in the past, it's obviously important to give some attention to the importance of "Forgiveness Time." In his book, *Forgive and Forget*, Lewis Smedes wrote, "When you release the wrongdoer from the wrong, you cut a malignant tumor out of your inner life. You set a prisoner free, but you discover that the real prisoner was yourself."

I mean, face it. People are *always* going to mess up, and occasionally, big time. How you react to these bumps in the road is up to you. When you hold on to hatred or become vindictive, you are totally setting yourself up for bad times. Likewise, when you choose to accept and forgive, you're setting up a wholly different response from the Universe. I mean, the karmic dance is real, people . . . and if you haven't figured it out yet, look again: *What goes around comes around.*

Implied in the popular *and* powerful Serenity Prayer is the understanding that you can't control other people's behavior . . . you can only control your own. So, when someone acts—beyond your control—in a way that you wish they hadn't, you can wisely accept the fact of their having done so, and you can *also* become willing to forgive their undesirable act and its influence on you . . . and thereby more quickly come back to a state of serenity *and* freedom from either reacting unhealthily toward them or harboring resentment in your heart. (There's a saying often heard in 12-Step recovery meetings: "Holding onto anger is like drinking poison and expecting the other person to die.")

In other words, if I really "get" that my family, friends, co-workers and everyone else I encounter are *bound* to make mistakes on a daily basis (as am I), and that I *cannot* control when or to what extent those mistakes will affect me or my interests, I'd be better off having a well-exercised "forgiveness muscle" to bring to the table when such inevitable events occur.

Years ago, I had a really bad breakup with an old boyfriend. It was a full-out war. As time went on, I had so much hatred for him that it was literally eating me up inside. I was losing weight like crazy, not sleeping, crying all the time and turning into a basket case. One day, I thought to myself, *That's it, I've had enough.*

Somehow, someway, I found the strength to call him up, ask him to dinner and sit across from him and forgive him, forgive myself and ask for peace. Once I went through with this, it felt like a gorilla had climbed off my back. To this day, he tells me he is floored by my having done what I did that night. In forgiving him, I set him free and myself free. I knew we weren't going to date again, so why hold on to the bad memories? Today, he is one of my best friends. The moral of the story? Everyone wins when you forgive. (At least, *you* do and oftentimes the other person, as well.)

I want to point out I'm not saying you are going to (or you ought to) forget when someone has wronged you in some way. But forgiving that person falls into the category of "higher level thinking." When someone is able to forgive, it shows me they're able to really see more angles of the situation than just what is there at face value. A broader perspective is being entertained. Clearly, there could be a million reasons why someone did what they did. Who are we to judge them?

When you forgive, you're actually using your ability to rise above the mud from which that person's "sin" was born ("sin" being a false idea about "what's real"). That is, forgiveness is rising up to see the falsity the person was—in that moment—living by and letting it go . . . holding instead to what's true: *Everyone of us carries around false ideas, including me—and since the truth of who I am and who they are essentially includes an infinite potential for more good to come from me or them, let's hold that vision in our awareness and move on.*

Another, slightly different angle on the topic of forgiveness is: *Hate breeds more hate* and *Love breeds love.* When you "hate" another person, you are doing the opposite of helping them. You're shooting them down in your mind and heart, actually pushing them in the wrong direction (i.e., stimulating feelings of defensiveness, rather than openness to being accepted—regardless of their mistaken perceptions—and inspired to change . . .), ultimately leading to more bad behavior.

On the other hand, how differently do people respond when they completely fuck up and you are *still* able to find it in your heart and soul to accept them, to forgive them, to love them. That is pretty much the opposite of what most people do and when I see it happen, it's almost shocking.

What we're looking at here is a pervasive reality in our society: *Anger and bitterness enslave us.* But you *can* stop and ask yourself: "How is that serving me?" It is *such* a gross feeling and it causes not only emotional problems, but physical issues. The mind/body connection is so strong, holding onto anger—instead of using acceptance and forgiveness as tools for achieving freedom and serenity—will literally make you sick.

Speaking of tools, this might sound nuts, but I pray for people who do bad things to me. The way I see it, they must be in a really bad place or quite desperate to stoop so low as to do me wrong. And I know in my heart and soul that my prayers and positive thinking will energetically help them and inevitably lift them up.

Another question I sometimes ask myself is: "Wouldn't *I* want forgiveness?" Go ahead, try and recall a time when you did or said something that hurt someone . . . then go a little further in your reflection and identify whether or not you wanted to be forgiven by the friend or family member who was then holding a grudge toward you. Seriously, an unresolved resentment or the lack of forgiveness in a relationship disrupts everything and makes everyone feel like total crap.

One thing I see over and over is women holding onto visceral pain from past relationships, then making their "current" boyfriend/husband suffer. Um, *not good*. That, my friends, is not going to work in your favor. If you catch yourself doing this, take stock of what you specifically need to let go of from that last relationship . . . and do it! Identify and then choose to release those particular residual hurts, pains and/or fears . . . for both your own and his sake!

In the end, if life gets way too heavy and you can't forgive on your own, I strongly suggest you run, don't walk, to your favorite therapist . . . and start talking. Talk about the issue 'til it is no longer an issue. Chant, meditate, do a juice cleanse— *whatever* it takes to let it goooooooo! Set yourself free. Anger and resentment are *not* our friends. They will hurt us (and possibly kill us via cancer, dis-ease, etc.), by keeping us stuck in the past . . . which blows . . . 'cuz us enlightened girls want to play in the present!

ENLIGHTENMENT IS SEXY CHAPTER TOOLBOX

Set Yourself Free With Forgiveness

Pray for people that do you wrong.
They obviously need it.

When you "hate" others or hold on to bad
feelings, you are only hurting yourself.

If you just can't get past something, get your
therapist on speed dial and deal with it.

13 Thinking is Over-rated: Escape Your Mental Prison

"It's dark because you are trying too hard. Lightly child, lightly. Learn to do everything lightly."

— *Aldous Huxley, Island*

What are thoughts? Have you ever pondered that question? According to the Merriam-Webster dictionary, a thought is: "an idea, plan, opinion, picture, etc. that is formed in your mind; something that you think of." Great, *so where do they come from?* My sense is thoughts are what occur when you combine experience and understanding, and mix them together with a dash of emotion. That is, thoughts reflect a combo platter of all of the "stuff" swirling around in your head you've picked up in your life, inclusive of the most recent moment's experience. *And*, when you toss in desire, fear, love, hope, greed—or any other type of emotion or mood—you spontaneously cook up "thoughts."

Quite often, thoughts amount to conclusions that *feel* real. But, from an objective standpoint, they can be ridiculously disconnected from reality. We have probably all had the experience, someone doesn't call you back or you don't get a response to a heartfelt email and all of a sudden you think to yourself, "Oh my God, he/she totally doesn't care about me anymore. They don't even want to talk to me!" Then a couple of weeks go by and you get an apologetic call from your friend, saying that something insane happened in their lives and they totally spaced out on getting back to you. You had made up some huge story in your mind, but the reality is that he/she just got side-tracked.

So listen up! If you let your thoughts rule your life—especially "out of touch with reality" thoughts or "downer" thoughts ("I'm fat" or "I'm ugly" or "I don't have enough money in the bank to feel safe," for example)—you'll quickly end up with the gift that keeps on giving; anxiety, depression, dis-ease, and complete lack of "presence," all of which lead you straight down the road of unhappiness.

The fact is, the thoughts in your mind aren't everything. You have an entire *Universe* you can tap into, which can enhance your life experience *at any moment you choose to plug into it.* I often say, "I don't really think." People laugh when I say that, but it's true. I tend to follow my gut, because I've come to realize my thoughts tend to get in the way. My inner guide, my intuition, my connection to the Universe's impulses, *that's* really running the show for *me.*

But you know, for *centuries* our society has been teaching us to value our intellect more than our intuition.

Use your mind to create a happy life.
Obey the rules.
Listen to your parents.
Get good grades.
Be a good girl.
Go to a good college.
Get a good job.
Done! Livin' the dream, right?

I say, *Wrong!* You see, if you follow these rules—because they're *thought* to produce results that'll make you happy—you'll very likely end up disconnected from your soul's passion and miserable at a core level!

I'm not saying, "Throw out the intellect"—not at all! But from what I can tell, it's a "tool" of our mind that's meant to serve us, rather than a master that enslaves us.

I think it's important to consider the following: these days, most any decent college requires a boatload of cash . . . and when you graduate, there are still no guarantees you will land *any* job, let alone your dream job. And, heck, most 18-year-olds have no clue what they want, so why does it make sense to go straight to college after high school, anyway? Just so you can—when you're not studying—drink beer, chase guys (or girls) and acquire very little life experience? What if, instead, you took a year off, took some of that "saved for college money" and traveled the world? Or tried out an internship? Or, if you really wanted to get wild, took some time just to figure out who you are and what you want to do in this life of yours?

In other words, find yourself.

Oh, the horror!

I didn't go to college right away. I took 8 months off, got a job in the city, and rented my own apartment *purposely* to study the art of living. Landing a great job and a killer place to live in a great part of Chicago brought me tremendous pride, given I was just fresh out of high school. Everyone else I knew went away to college, joined sororities or fraternities, drank their asses off for 4 years and then joined the workforce. By the time I started college, I knew I wanted to be a comparative religious studies major. I felt strongly that God and how people view spirituality around the world was the most important topic I could study.

Looking back, I can see how amazing it was that I chose Comparative Religious Studies as my major. As I reflect on where I'm at now, it's clear that spirituality is the most important part of my life. I know organized religion and spirituality are different, but I was already showing signs of major interest in "consciousness" and different ways of experiencing it. THIS WAS NOT RANDOM.

What I believe is this: *Finding yourself is way more important than finding facts and figures.*

While my father was happy his daughter was going to be a college graduate (the first in our family), he was NOT thrilled with my impractical, "irrational" choice of major. I came from a family of entrepreneurs—all successful business owners— and none of them went to school. They used their drive and intuition to persevere. When I graduated, I was ironically working for my dad at one of his restaurants. So, about 100 thousand dollars later, that degree, while interesting, really didn't move me forward in the workforce. Pretty crazy, when you think about it. This reality hit me on the first day I started meditating. I explained to people that in 20 minutes of meditating, I knew more about what's important in life than I did going to college for four years.

What's my point? We are all born with knowledge and intuition. It's built into our DNA. Our souls are made up of wisdom that can carry us throughout our lives. The problem is, our society doesn't teach us to cultivate our intuition and definitely doesn't show us how to rely on it. But that's what I'm suggesting we do, every day, as often as possible!

The irony in all of this is that it's your intuition that will carry you through your life. This goes back to the theory that we *are* being carried. The Universe, by its own nature, leads us forward, supports our growth and expansion of awareness . . . *all* of us . . . *always*. Each day, we meet new people, have new experiences, and make new decisions. Wouldn't life be so much easier to just follow your intuition about all of it? The fact is, if you want to make use of it, your "inner wizard" (aka intuition) is there to guide you every step of the way. As you get better and better at this, you can start depending on it, full-time. Soon, it will become obvious to you that we are all created with this super inner intelligence (again, your intuition) that *won't* let you down. On the journey of life, it is your friend, your partner and the ultimate guru.

When I gave my first lengthy talk about meditation on my own and was representing my new company, I remember being nervous as all hell. Although my anxious thoughts were making me question why I was there and doubt my unworthiness to talk about anything to anyone, I decided my thoughts were *not* going to run the show. In an instant, I told myself, *I'm just going to speak from my heart. Period!*

I got up and preached like I had never preached before. Hallelujah! I deeply connected with my audience, and the words I spoke felt completely channeled. It was amazing, and it changed my world. (Indeed, what I shared that day was super well-received by the audience!)

From that day onward, "not thinking" became my new way of living. Sure, it seemed strange at first, but after a while I realized my mind just wasn't that compelling any more. My soul took the wheel, and my instincts shifted the gears. Together, they drove my train on a life-affirming path forward. *Everything* began to work *and* to work out. I noticed EVERYTHING around me. The birds' songs brought the trees to life, and I found outrageous joy in just taking a walk. "Feeling" everything around me made life truly exciting and full. It was obvious to me I was being led by something way bigger than myself, and this "other" thing had plans way cooler for me than I'd ever "thought" of.

I'd like to point out, too, that the saying, "You are not your thoughts," is not some hippy-dippy idea—it's an actual experience. When I gave that first talk to Oprah and a few of her top executives, if I would have depended solely on my mind, I would have lost it. What was actually happening is that I was "witnessing" my thoughts. I was solid in my silence and it seemed as though I was just watching the words come out of my mouth (hence, the term "witnessing"). I was unshakable . . . and that is the ONLY reason a powerful person like Oprah would even notice me. I was absolutely working from a "higher level of consciousness." I just had never experienced that before, and it seems totally crazy that it happened to me the first time I got up and spoke in front of one of the most powerful women in the country, if not the world.

When I started using this obviously different "not thinking" approach in my life (on a consistent basis, that is), one of my first questions was, "Why aren't more people talking about *not* depending so wholly on your intellect?" I mean, why is this such a foreign concept to us? I began to wonder, "Could this be part of the reason there is so much unhappiness in the world?" I've concluded it's a very real possibility. If the majority of people are operating within a system that really doesn't work (i.e., thinking one's way to a happy life), why would we expect the results to be fruitful and fulfilling?

Ultimately, I asked myself, *How can we dismantle and then replace this system in which we have been brought up?*

Silence is a good start. Just sitting and being quiet will help you tap into your innate inner wisdom. Practicing daily meditation (TM or whatever technique suits you) can connect you to your inner GPS, the "Cosmic Computer," freeing you up from your predisposition to "think your way" through life.

And hey, have fun with it! If you wake up in the morning and feel a strong urge to call a certain someone (even if you haven't spoken with them in years) or to get in your car and drive to a new town, *do it!* Start out slowly and see what happens. Over time, you'll likely find this "intuitive approach" will spill over into your everyday decision-making. In this regard, you can only learn through experience, so start getting some!

You see, it has been drilled into our minds that we have to operate a certain way, but "who" are we really listening to? Look at the people around you, the people who've shaped you. Are they happy and fulfilled? Most importantly, how are they living? If you admire them and want to be like them, then imitate them. But, if you want to do it differently, you'll likely need to make some significant changes. However, I believe *nothing* is more fulfilling than following your own path. Marching to your own drum. This serendipitous, synchronistic, magical "stuff" that starts to fill you up and pervade your life comes from *inside* of you. You find you're being fed answers to all your questions, given good directions towards all your dreams and offered up gifts that will help the world become a better place.

Commit to listening much more often to your soul's inner voice, and to relying upon your intuition. Treat it like a rare diamond and cherish it. It will not fail you, and will only make you stronger. It's your connection to the Universal mind that runs through every living thing in this world. Tap into it and you'll be tapping into pure life force.

And next time someone says to you, "Start using your head," respond back to them, "No, thank you. I have a different plan. I'm gonna' use my soul."

'Cuz, let's be honest, your soul knows WAY more than your head could ever conceive.

ENLIGHTENMENT IS SEXY CHAPTER TOOLBOX

Thinking Is Overrated

Start relying on your intuition

Do the opposite of what you have been told. Get out of your head and into your gut level.

Become connected to your inner silence. That's where all the juice comes from. It's like a tree—the roots are the silence, the trunk is the intuition and the leaves (which fall) are your thoughts. Everything grows from silence. Water the root, mother-fuckers!

14

Becoming a Master at Manifesting

"You have to participate relentlessly in the manifestation of your own blessings."

—Elizabeth Gilbert

Did you know that thoughts become things? Since thoughts are made of energy, and what you give energy to grows, your thoughts—what you focus your attention on—eventually becomes your reality . . . *whether you realize it or not.*

When you look backwards, you can perhaps see that where you are *right now* in life has crossed your mind at some point in the past. Maybe not all the specific details, but how about the general scenario? And what does that teach us? Well, it's evidence that the Universe actually works backwards. You heard me. *Backwards.* Finish to start. You have the thought and then you are "led" to the end result. That is, within the vast array of thoughts in the ocean of your consciousness, you're already seeing your future—then through a series of so-called coincidences, synchronicities and nudges, you end up right where you "thought" you would be.

Now, you might be asking yourself, "Wait a second! I dreamt of being a millionaire by the time I was 25, but I'm broke as a joke! How did that happen?!?"

I'll tell you what very likely happened:

a. You probably just weren't ready to have "X." That is, you hadn't finished all your spiritual "homework" in order to have "X" going on in your life. (The bottom line? The Universe's time schedule is the only working clock in this house.)

b. You didn't believe deep down you're really worthy of having "X."

c. You didn't solely focus on the end result.
d. You got caught up in the "how" (as in, "I'm sure *this* is how I make such-and-such happen").
e. You didn't spend sufficient time "feeling" (i.e., in advance) the feelings you'd have when your desire *has* been manifested.

See, the Universe isn't interested in "your way." It already *knows* what to do. And It's only interested in what you want. Period.

"Say what?!" Again, you're probably left wondering, "So what *is* my responsibility in manifesting what I want?"

Well, it's actually simple. These are the 4 steps I recommend to become a "master manifester":

1. Visualize the end result (clearly identify what you really want).
2. Spend some time each day feeling the feelings you'd naturally experience when reaching your final destination.
3. Take action (whatever your vision and intuition guide you to do), so you're constantly moving towards your dream (the desired end result).
4. Expect success—act as though you're *already* your "future self," the one enjoying that end result.

Following these steps with consistency and commitment will help you manifest whatever you really want. How do I know this? *It's been my experience . . .* and it's what I've observed in countless inspiring, successful people I've admired over the years.

There is another piece to this puzzle, though. An extremely important part of this "Cosmic Game" is that you have to take massive action towards actually becoming your future self. Everyday moving towards that new reality, being that person your dreams are calling you to be.

When *The Secret* came out, I was super-psyched, because "magical thinking" (i.e., how to manifest your desires) suddenly was becoming mainstream. But they left out a necessary, essential component: *action in the forward direction*. Without forward motion, your dreams are *not* going to become your reality.

The Universe knows what you want and is just waiting for you to get in line with your heart's truest desires. It's simple, yes . . . and no, we're not being smart if we sit around all day in our sweatpants trying to *will* the Universe to create some supreme reality for us. This is a *partnership*: we are working hand-in-hand with a Higher Power (whatever we understand It to be, whatever we choose to call It), so we have to keep up our side of the bargain . . . which is to tune into our desires and feel them being *already* fulfilled (by the Universe).

Do you think it's a coincidence most lottery winners[3] lose all the cash they've won in a relative blink

---

3 According to a NY Times article, 90% of all U.S. lottery winners go broke within 5 years. http://bucks.blogs. nytimes.com/2012/12/03/a-financial-plan-for-misbehaving-lottery-winners/?_r=0

of an eye? Why do you think this happens? I have a theory: They simply weren't ready for a boatload of cash to hit their bank account and they explode. Family members and friends come out of the wood-work with their hands out, spending spins out of control—because the money wasn't earned—and really, most lotto winners just didn't make it a prior-ity to prepare themselves *internally* for such a huge lifestyle shift.

The bottom line is this: we *all* have to really ready ourselves for our desires to manifest *or else things won't turn out as planned.* Even worse, it could be a disaster . . . and homie don't play that game.

I can remember being a teenager and read-ing authors like Wayne Dyer and Louise Hay, all the while quietly dreaming of becoming a spiritual teacher. I would get glimpses of my future, but at the time those visions were so far out of range from how I was living, there wasn't a chance in hell I was going to step into those shoes!

That being said, I never stopped reading metaphysical and sacred texts or exploring the "otherworldly realm" I felt so connected to. Still, although I was committed to expanding my interior world, my exterior world was telling a much differ-ent story. I lived to go to the next party, date the next cute guy who crossed my path, or travel to the latest hot spot. *Nothing* was matching up, so my desires remained pie-in-the-sky dreams.

Obviously, I wasn't ready to move into my destiny.

But after my mom died and my world went black, something major shifted. My "old" life was over, and I never was to return to my crazy "good time Charlie" ways. I was on a new path . . . a deeply spiritual road of transformation, higher levels of consciousness and service to my truth. At first I wasn't really clear on what I was going to do, but slowly I started moving toward the vision I'd had earlier in life: I wanted to live in the spiritual world full-time. *This is the work I was born to do*, I thought, and finally my exterior reality began connecting with my interior world.

Almost without thought, I began feeling motivated to start writing down my thoughts, strengthen my meditation practice, clean up my diet and start living a quieter lifestyle. I can see now my following through on all these decisions led me to who I am today. Before I knew it I had written this book, created an Enlightenment Is Sexy blog, started a web design company and entered into a brand new reality. Except it wasn't "brand new." It just seemed that way. I have held this desire in my mind and soul since I was 13 years old. Finally, it became my reality.

Working towards my dreams has become a pleasure. I can see the layers of action that need to be taken to fulfill my desires and I just step into that movement. Every day, I walk right into my untouched reality. Doors open and I walk through them. I am owning my destiny, because I have now experienced the nuts and bolts of manifesting. You *can* have your cake and eat it too, *but first you must become the real deal.*

> "Therefore I say unto you, what things soever ye desire,when ye pray, believe that ye receive them, and ye shall have them."
> —Jesus Christ (Mark 11:24, *The Bible*)

You are manifesting all day, everyday. Every action you take, every thought you have and every prayer you whisper has energy. Think of a giant grid in the sky. Every time you have a desire, it gets added to the grid. It's as though this network of thoughts is collected up somehow and added to the Universe's hard drive. This "ultimate brain trust" is listening to your heart's wishes and dreams, and in turn is giving you clues all day, leading you to your own personal Promised Land. *Your* job is to get yourself into a position where you can "hear" the guidance.

Spiritual practices make us ninjas in this department. Silence and contemplative reflection allow the mind, body and spirit to tap into this detailed "spiritual being user's manual" that will show you the way. All of us have the opportunity to be and do anything we want—it just takes a whole lot of guts and an open channel to the Universe's signs and guidance.

157

Rumi wasn't kidding when he said what you seek is seeking you. It's like everything is backwards. We have the thought and then the Universe starts walking towards it . . . *but the thought itself is not random.* They are winks from your future self nudging you along. It's the reason some people fantasize about climbing Mt. Everest and the person next to them dreams of becoming a mother. We are all walking towards our true destiny, but learning the lessons and doing the work is up to us. Everything you desire is waiting for you. It is your birthright to live the life of your dreams. We all just need a little planning and a whole lot of vibration-raising action steps. Fall in love with the process and eventually the magic will start flowing.

So, here's my take on "summarizing what's important" for all you "manifesters-in-the-making":

1. Visualize like a mother-trucker. Keep your eye on the prize and actually become your future self. *Now.*
2. Write out in detail what you want for yourself. Look at that list. *Every single day.*
3. Get honest with yourself. If you hate your life (or even if you don't *like* something about it), *change it.* Walk right into the fire. You will be rewarded in gold.
4. Ride the waves of life. When things start going your way, *keep going.* Flow is the key to this carnival ride.

5. Spiritual practice? Yes. Do some homework, ask the best questions you can, and then pick up a spiritual practice you feel aligned with. Ultimately, regular spiritual practice will give you the ability to really tap into the Universe's ways.

Once you get going, you'll eventually gain momentum. Really, you will. You'll start to notice things *are* going your way, and life *is* becoming a little lighter. You'll feel carried. That's the Universe giving you the green light. *Keep going.* Your dreams are just around the bend.

ENLIGHTENMENT IS SEXY CHAPTER TOOLBOX

Becoming a Master at Manifesting

(See #1 - #5 directly above)

15 Seek Truth in Meditation

"To the mind that is still,
the whole universe surrenders."

—Lao Tzu

For those of you may have never explored meditation yourselves, *and* because there are so many widely varying approaches to meditation now being taught worldwide, I want to give you a detailed, personal account of what it was like for me to learn meditation . . . and why it's something I'd strongly suggest you consider as a way to enhance every aspect of your life.

As I recounted in the second chapter ("Once Upon a Time"), following my mother's death I found myself in the deepest, darkest valley of my life. For nearly thirteen years, I'd practically lived in hospitals with her—the woman I'd counted as my best friend, closest confidante and my guru—as she dealt with cancer and ultimately her own death. Not long before she passed, recognizing how much I was struggling, my mom handed me a bottle of pills and said, "Here, you're going to need these."

Thoroughly numbing my pain, any joy I might have occasionally glimpsed back then, and every sensation in between, those pills worked like a charm—that is, until they didn't any more. I was also losing my ongoing battle with a debilitating sleep disorder (which had intensified over the previous few years) -- and if you've ever gone days at a time without sleeping, you know the bat-shit crazy thoughts a serious lack of sound slumber brings. Depression had slowly begun to invade my days and nights, gradually destroying me, and suicidal thoughts were creeping around in the darkness of my mind.

One evening, one of my dearest guy friends—who I know was worried about me, at the time—invited me to a dinner party, during which I had my first conversation about meditation, Transcendental Meditation (TM), to be exact. I remember who I was that night: a woman coming desperately unraveled, trudging through each and every day with such deep sadness I could hardly describe it.

Drowning in a puddle at a table surrounded by ten guys (all of them power traders), I hadn't even bothered to brush my hair. There I sat, crying into my pinot noir, as these men shot the breeze at an industry dinner. One of them was kind enough to ask me what was wrong.

"How do you feel? What are you thinking?"

Perhaps because I'd fallen so far, I opened my shattered heart up to him and laid it bare on the table for him to see. I told him everything: how I hadn't slept properly in thirteen years, how I didn't know who I was or what was happening, how I didn't think I was going to make it. I neglected to tell him I'd planned on giving away my dog to a cousin who lived in another state and chosen not to get a new car once the lease on mine was up, because a woman on a mission to off herself in the near future doesn't need a dog or a car. That is, I had completely abandoned all hope.

He explained to me and the friend who'd invited me to the party why I should learn how to meditate as soon as possible, and where I could go to learn a highly regarded form of it. My friend took down all of the basic information, and we both thanked this "angel in disguise" for his genuine care and kindness.

The following day, my friend called Carla, the local Transcendental Meditation teacher, and made an appointment for me to meet her. He also paid for my instruction, lent me his car, and a few days later, I went for my first consultation.

Mind you, I had zero understanding of what meditation was, nor did I care. I'd descended so deeply into depression, anxiety and isolation that I was willing to try anything. (It certainly helped that my sweet friend was going to foot the bill.)

The process of learning how to do TM consisted of four days of instruction, around 1½ hours per day. Once we'd sat down, Carla whispered the mantra she'd selected for me and then explained how to use it in meditation, guiding me to experience the effortless nature of the TM form of meditation. Within five minutes, I got it. Sitting together in *complete* silence—a silence I had never experienced before—I understood more about life, God, and my soul after meditating for 20 minutes than I ever did studying world religion in college for four years. The process blew the roof off of my mind and released an internal volcano of intelligence. At first, I repeated the mantra in my mind as my only thought. Soon, I had no thoughts. Zero, zip, nothing.

My mind locked arms with my soul, and the frazzled, heartbroken woman I had been was gone. Uniting with a wiser, higher part of my "Self" I hadn't ever met before, I touched the palm of God that day. When I opened my eyes after 20 minutes, I saw the world through a new Technicolor lens. Everything was brighter, the air felt softer, and even the sound of children fighting coming in from the open window where I was meditating sounded like a sweet reminder I was alive.

What the hell is going on? I wondered. *How could this be?!? Twenty minutes ago, I was ready to jump off a building, and now I'm living in a dream . . . a beautiful and vibrant cocoon of love.*

"Trippy" doesn't even *begin* to explain what was happening in my mind. I told my teacher I would see her the next day and that I was going home to take a nap. I jumped into the beast of a sports car I had borrowed and drove down Lake Shore Drive, marveling at how the streets of Chicago had morphed into a Monet painting. What I felt certainly defies words: "amazing" doesn't really do it justice, but I felt utterly amazed by all of life.

When I got home, I passed out into a fantastically deep sleep. My head hit the pillow and I didn't move for 13 straight hours. I mean, I basically slept until my next appointment with Carla. I hadn't slept like that since high school! This was the type of sleep people only *dream* of. Obviously, the meditation had primed me to get rid of a huge amount of fatigue I'd stored up. Once I got up out of it, though, I felt like a new person.

On my second day of meditation instruction, after Carla asked me some questions, we sat down to meditate again. Both a Christ-like figure and a 40-year-old healthy and happy version of my mother approached me during my meditation that day. They just appeared in front of me, almost close enough to touch. There was no ground below them and no ceiling above them. Just the two figures floating in front of my eyes. They were communicating with me through our minds, and telling me everything was okay. My mom was not only safe, but she was with Christ. *And I could see them!* Holy Christmas!!! *This was wild.*

Though I'd never told anyone, the reason I had wanted to kill myself after my mother's death was that I had it in my head she needed me—that she was looking for me, because she was confused. The fact that I had no idea where she was or if she was safe drove me mad.

Well, as insane as this "vision" (of my mom and Christ) sounds (and seemed to me), I didn't feel afraid. I felt completely connected to everything— all of life—and most importantly to my mother, who was so clearly content in "heaven."

I told my teacher how I felt and what I saw that day. Without skipping a beat, she smiled at me and said, "This is really going to change your life." Little did I know, that was the understatement of the century.

Extraordinary things just began happening to me, and I mean quickly—like some subtle stroke of Divine intervention. In fact, that serendipitous dinner party had been the impetus for the best thing that has ever happened to me. Within two months of learning TM, I began working with the David Lynch Foundation, helping the teachers who instructed Oprah Winfrey's entire staff in TM. I slept every single night, never took another Xanax and became, for lack of a better phrase, a *deeply* happy person.

Transcendental Meditation honed my mind in a way that generated newfound energy in me and a pure sense of excitement for life. It is now the backbone of my spiritual practices. I have meditated every day since that first day—twice a day, twenty minutes in the morning and twenty minutes in the early evening. This practice keeps my soul sound, my mind clear and my heart close to God.

As a sort of side note, I'd like to mention something I consider out-the-roof amazing about my having specifically learned TM.

The fact is, almost a year after my mom passed and 9 months after I learned TM, I was sitting down having dinner with my father. By now he had become very familiar with meditation and my new work. Many of our family members and friends had learned TM and, one by one, they kept reporting back to my father things like, "Your daughter has got something good going on . . . and that TM she suggested I check out has actually changed my life." He didn't completely understand, but he was super-supportive.

Since everyone who learned TM who'd spoken with my dad had been required to attend four days in a row of instruction (that's the way it's taught), he started picking up on these four-day blocks of time both they and I were often referring to . . . and at this particular dinner, it finally hit him.

"You know, Val, back in the seventies, I took your mom to a house in suburban Chicago, I think it was Oak Park, four days in a row, so she could learn how to meditate."

I almost fell over, although my dad didn't seem to think it was a big deal.

My mom was a TM'er, just like me.

But it gets even wilder.

I immediately called my friend Wally and explained the story to him. He told me there are records at the National TM Office of every person who had ever learned TM in the U.S. And so within a day, I had proof that my mom had learned TM on December 6, 1975.

I did the math and quickly realized she had unexpectedly gotten pregnant with me a month later.

Not only did my mom meditate, but she meditated *while I was in her belly.*

I was a born meditator. Literally.

I believe we all have a different path, a road upon which we drive. The path leads us over mountains to horizons flooded with beauty and joy, through sorrow-filled valleys and everywhere in between. I am so grateful that TM was one of my pit stops, during which I got a "tool" that seems to be steadily expanding my consciousness and providing me with what I need to enjoy the very best life I could possibly have.

TM is what worked for me. Who knows what's right for you, but I encourage you to pick up *some* spiritual practice that feels like it's the "right fit" for where you're at in your life.

For more information on Transcendental Meditation, go to www.tm.org. It is a great site with tons of information and instructions on how to connect with a TM teacher near you.

ENLIGHTENMENT IS SEXY CHAPTER TOOLBOX

Seek Truth In Meditation

(This chapter has no "toolbox," other than . . .)
. . . *Start meditating*—if you aren't already
doing so—that way, you can stop being an
out of control head-tripper and begin living
the magical life you were born to have!

16

Destroy What No Longer Works for You

"When a problem comes along,
you must whip it. Whip it good."

—Devo

We all know how it goes: you think to yourself, *If only I could get my shit together, life would be so much cooler.* Well, you're right. Your entire life *would* be smoother, richer and much lighter if you could *eliminate what doesn't work for you anymore.* The big question is, "Where to start?" I believe a wise first step would be to identify what is *really* going on in the important dimensions of your life (self/well-being, significant relationships, career, etc.), because quite often, what you *think* is the problem is not the *actual* problem.

The fact is, there is always something inside of you that drives you to act in a certain way. Low self-worth could be the cause of letting people walk all over you. Anxiety could be driving you to drink a bottle of wine every night. In other words, one thing leads to another. You have to really take a hard look at what is happening in your life to get at the essential reason this or that problem exists in the first place. WHY are you doing what you are doing? Pay attention to the patterns. A hard day at work flows into coming home and drinking that bottle of wine, which flows into you feeling like crap the next day, which flows into having a harder time at work again, and on and on we go. Pay attention and watch your patterns. That sort of awareness, in my opinion, is a *necessary* first step in changing them.

When you start taking care of yourself on a spiritual level (e.g., through regular meditation, prayer, personal growth practices), some of your problems will just dissolve on their own. It's part of the magic of becoming "centered." When you become more connected to the laws of nature that are running the entire universe, you begin to act accordingly—you *naturally* won't abuse yourself or others, because it will no longer work for you.

I'll give you an example. Remember that sleeping disorder I mentioned that practically took me out? Once I started meditating and released whatever stress was causing the issue, it just went away. These days, I *never, ever* think about "not sleeping." It's just not part of my reality, anymore. That's how it works. Once you get to the heart of "why" issues are popping up, you can smash them.

Now, just because you start up with a spiritual practice and begin feeling better, that doesn't mean all of your crap just magically disappears. You'll still have to work at resolving whatever past behaviors, beliefs and attitudes that have been keeping you limited or locked in to frustrating, self-defeating patterns -- but by enlivening the spiritual dimension of your life, you'll begin seeing your problems with an expanded consciousness, which makes working things out a *hell* of a lot easier.

You might be wondering, "Once we've identified the essential nature of our problems, how do we move past them . . . and then 'destroy them' once and for all?"

This is what worked for me. As soon as I got centered in my meditation practice, got my mind back in order and climbed out of my fog, I got a plan of attack in order. I wasn't interested in spiritually bypassing my earthly issues. I wanted to walk straight into the fire and look my "roadblocks" right in the eye. I made a choice to really just "stop, drop and roll."

Step 1 - Sit down and write it all down. Every single issue, fear, self-defeating belief, repeating pattern, unhealthy vice, whatever you're dealing with. Personally, I had 10 pages (just to show you where I began).

Step 2 - Write down *why* you think you're still holding on to behaviors that no longer serve you. As you write, become intimate with your most messed up self. Own it.

Step 3 - Come up with a solid plan to move past each particular issue and become the strong woman you were put on this earth to be. For me, I decided, on top of continuing with my newly learned meditation practice, I would go talk with a therapist for 6 months and really dig deep. I was going to face the music, no matter how bad it hurt.

Step 4 - Take massive action. Whatever you've planned and whatever it takes to get your life in order, start doing it. And then don't stop 'til you feel satisfied with your life!

I believe "problems" are the Universe's way of waking us up and encouraging us to pay attention to our lives. We actually *need* them to help us grow. Now, when I find myself in challenging situations, I just know it's time to grow a little more. I actually look forward to situations I know will push me. Of course, I'm not *hoping* bad things will happen to me or anyone, but it *is* a natural part of life. Sometimes you're up, and sometimes you're down. Without the problems that temporarily bring you "down," how else are you going to learn about your latent strengths and opportunities to expand yourself? So, why not start practicing more acceptance and less resistance (and complaining)?

Ultimately, "acceptance" and "rolling with it" makes life so much easier to navigate. When you operate on this level of understanding, the challenging circumstances in front of you are no longer "bad"—they're just the Universe nudging you forward.

Just as importantly, there's obviously no point— at least in my mind—in ignoring my crap. It's not going to go anywhere, and it just makes life hard. We *are* in control of our attitude toward-. . . well, everything in our lives, which ultimately means we're in charge of our own happiness. When I face the things in front of me (or within me), I can make progress in resolving or dissolving whatever I don't want to live with any longer. But if, instead, I let myself remain fearful and hide from or ignore those same things, it's very likely I'll continue to be plagued and imprisoned by them.

Once I've identified my problems clearly and developed and begun acting on a plan to resolve them, one by one, these problems begin to disappear, to the point where I may not even notice they were ever there. They become like a faint memory: "Oh yeah, I remember when I did that."

If you persist in taking positive action toward releasing whatever doesn't serve you, the problem will eventually disappear. With some diligent work on your part, you'll smooth out the transition. Sure, you're likely to hit a few bumps in the road, but then you'll get good at it. You'll see clearly that something isn't good for you and *you just won't do it anymore.* You won't be tortured by it or have a fear of missing out. Instead, it will just be part of an increasingly smooth ride, like the rest of your life. That is what we want, to be smooth as butter.

So when life gets heavy, keep Julius Caesar's famous quote in your mind, *"Veni, vidi, vici* (I came, I saw, I conquered)." BOOM!

In fact, as you strengthen your centeredness and you feel you possess a truly empowered sense of self in your daily life, you can actually crush any problem that comes your way, as they arise. Obstacles that, in the past, *could* get in the way of your happiness just can't take hold any longer. *You no longer play that game.* You now know you're able to *choose* your own mood and address this or that matter directly, effectively and efficiently.

On top of this, facing your problems and dealing with them *in the moment* will separate you from the herd, fueling you with a strength you've never before encountered. You begin to rise each day feeling and knowing the spiritual warrior within you is real, alive and ready for anything . . . and you know you have God as your co-pilot. That combo platter is *completely* unstoppable.

At the end of the day, we all need to face the music . . . and own up to our responsibility for creating the life and level of happiness we want. Once you become spiritually centered, one of the major challenges is learning (or relearning) how to live with the "truth." We need to develop fluency at living free of "other people's" structures and take the next step, then the next step, then the next step . . . into the unknown of our own life-to-be. I know it can be scary as hell, but walking your own path, the courageous pioneer's path forward is where all the *really* good stuff is.

What I mean is this: eventually, the veil of illusion gets lifted, and you need to retrain yourself to live by your own rules. Sure, it can be intense as hell, but I promise it is worth the ride. You *may* have the feeling you have no idea what is really going on for a while—but *that* will be your first great sign. It means you're feeling the shift. Then you will start making decisions that might seem a little crazy (especially to outsiders), e.g., quitting your (unsatisfying) job,

ending a longstanding (going-nowhere) relationship, and whatever else is no longer working for
you. But you couldn't possibly live your "old" life—
you are a different person! It will be obvious to you
that your past has to die before your future can
begin. Hence, you need to destroy what no longer
serves you! In short order, your spiritual awakening
will break you wide open and all I can is, "Hallelujah for that!" Because, trust me, that's one gift that
totally keeps on giving.

ENLIGHTENMENT IS SEXY CHAPTER TOOLBOX

Destroy What No Longer Works For You

(The Toolbox for this
chapter is in the 4 steps:)

Write down every issue, fear, vice, self-defeating belief or pattern you currently "have."

Write down why you think you're holding onto these, with the intention of getting to know and own your "dark side" more thoroughly.

Develop a plan to move past each issue, fear, etc. and become your truer, stronger self!

Take massive action in your
most desired direction.

17 Signs of Spiritual Awakening

"It isn't by getting out of the world that we become enlightened, but by getting into the world...by getting so tuned in that we can ride the waves of our existence and never get tossed, because we become the waves."

—Ken Kesey

When I learned to meditate and had an explosion of body, mind and soul in the first five seconds of closing my eyes, I knew almost instantly that my whole world was about to change. There was no denying something major had occurred and my life was about to get really interesting. (Actually, it was so intense and explosive, it took me about a year for my mind to catch up with my soul. To say "the times they are a-changin'" would have been the understatement of the year.

Very quickly, I realized I could no longer do the same things I was used to doing. I looked at my friends differently, I couldn't eat the same way I had for decades, I needed more time alone, and staying up and partying the night away was now completely out of the question. I can remember going out on the town one night with about 10 friends, shortly after I'd started meditating. The evening started like it always did, with dinner and drinks. I can remember sitting at the head of the table and feeling like I was totally separate from everyone around me. I felt very disconnected. We were at a BBQ restaurant and I remember feeling ill looking at all the meat. As the drinks flowed, though, I began to let go of all these thoughts in my head. After dinner, of course, we went to a bar and drank and laughed just like old times . . . except this time would be different. After staying out till 4 a.m., I came home and crashed. The next morning, I woke up and absolutely thought I was going to die! The alcohol hadn't agreed *at all* with me and I was literally hanging on for dear life! Something had radically changed and the something was *me*. From that day forward, I never touched another drop of hard alcohol. *I just couldn't do it anymore.* Without warning, my body had said, "That's it, I'm out!" But hard liquor intolerance would be just *one* of the changes I would go through. This former party girl was about to do a serious "180."

Looking back, I wasn't an easy fix. And really, I didn't want to believe I *had* changed, but there was no denying I had. The Universe just wouldn't let up. If I ate what had become "the wrong thing" (a hot fudge sundae or a deep-fried anything, for example), I got sick to my stomach. If I stayed up too late, I couldn't think the next day. If I hung around people who I really didn't like, I felt depressed. On and on it went. The point is, my "spiritual awakening" wasn't all rainbows and butterflies. I found that it's hard work to unlearn everything you've ever known. And with every turn I made, it seemed I was being guided (sometimes it seemed more like *steered*) by a force I wasn't in control of. *Great!* I thought on more than one occasion. *This is going to be one hell of a ride!*

Here are some of the changes I experienced:

1. **My Entire Belief System Changed:** As I mentioned before, when I learned to meditate I

realized everything I knew was wrong. My entire view on life changed. I had a very clear idea that what society was preaching was definitely fucked up, and by following that road you'd most likely be in for a hollow existence. And I quickly had another realization: I didn't need a middleman to get to God. I still knew that, for many, going to church or being part of an organized religion was, by and large, a good thing, but it no longer was completely necessary. My new sense of freedom allowed me to be in the driver's seat and my new co-pilot was the Universe itself.

2. **A Totally Different Career Path:** Up until the time I started meditating, I had spent my adult life in the bar and restaurant business. My goal had always been to open up a string of my own places. Actually, I was smack dab in the middle of opening my own bar when the Universe let me know "the plan" had changed. After I started working with my meditation teacher at Harpo Studios, I quickly realized I wanted to go in a completely different direction: to talk about spirituality, meditation and personal freedom for a living. I wanted to make a difference in the world and this was going to be the avenue I would use. Yeah, pretty damn different than serving Jaeger Bombs all night!

3. **A Newfound Love of Nature:** Trust me, I would have never considered myself a tree hugger,

prior to my awakening. I was more of a "slap on a kick ass gold cocktail dress, killer high heels and smoky eyes" kind of gal. Nature was just really not my thing. Living in the middle of Chicago, I didn't really get a chance to bond with the outdoors. But that was all about to change. Upon having my spiritual eyeballs opened wide, the one thing that really stood out for me was my newfound love of trees, the clouds and all flowers that crossed my path. I began experiencing an overwhelming sense that I am connected to all living things, including plants and animals. Staring at trees became my new pastime, and sometimes they would even talk back to me :)

4. **Synchronicities Galore:** "Magic" started happening everywhere. Unexpected connections, serendipitous events and all sorts of synchronicities began sprouting up all around me. It was so intense that I became (and am) convinced *the Universe is with me every move.* The question did arise, regarding this synchronicity situation: Was it always there and I just started noticing it? That thought ran through my mind 5 trillion times. Nevertheless, now I can look back and see the Universe's signs were, all along, guiding me straight into my best life. Talk about awesome!

5. **Serious Confusion:** I and my life had changed so rapidly, there *were* some really confusing times. I mean, when your whole world looks different

to you and no one around you is seeing what you're seeing, things are going to get a bit hairy. It can be hard to find support from people who don't "get" you, and that can make things even *more* puzzling. But, eventually I began to see things would just start working out in a different way. An alternative route—sometimes *quite* different than the one I "thought" I was on—would just appear in front of me. And *voila!* Life would roll forward, only in an unexpected, very often even more kick-ass way than I could have imagined! Yes, I can say without a shadow of a doubt, it's best to just hold steady and blow through the confusion till this new way of life becomes your new "normal."

6. **The Body Becomes A Temple:** I no longer could abuse my body. I found myself spontaneously changing the way I ate: no more late nights scarfing down pizza and drinking beer like it's water. No ma'am. Those days flew right out the window. Now, I look for food that's pure and can fuel my body. Green drinks have become my main squeeze, and fresh fruits and vegetables my posse. Eating poorly and not exercising is no longer an option. I have so much energy now, and I have to do something to get it out of my body. Daily long walks are now just part of my life. I don't even have to think about it, I just walk. And my dog sure is happy about *that* change!

7. **Less Is More:** After I began to wake up to this "new" world, I really had no use for lots of "stuff." So much of it felt more like a burden than a luxury. The result? Out went tons of my possessions. I sold all of my fancy shoes, purses, cocktail dresses and anything else I didn't feel I needed anymore. I gave away practically everything I couldn't fit in my car. That might sound extreme, but I'm telling you -- I have *never* felt so free in my life. Not only did I feel awesome giving away stuff I knew other people would love, I am over then moon that I can go wherever I want and don't have tons of crap holding me back. I'm down to 4 suitcases and my dog. Of course, this will change over the course of time . . . but for now, it sure feels like a fresh start. Ahhhhhhhhhhh!

8. **Sleep:** What happens once I lay down and close my eyes seems to take on a life of it's own. As soon as this new world opened up to me, my sleep changed . . . radically. I began to gather information while I slept (like it was being downloaded into my consciousness), I was able to connect with family members who had passed away, I need much less sleep than I used to, and the *most* interesting change has been there are nights when I would literally "watch myself" sleep (like I was a silent witness to it). This didn't scare or worry me, but I can assure you I *was*

outside of my body, just observing myself in bed. No thought, no emotion, just me and my peaceful body snoozing away. Now, most nights I sleep like a baby and I actually look forward to my nighttime adventures. They are always enlightening and often rather cosmic.

These are some of the changes I've experienced on my newfound path. Some have been rather wild and some have been challenging, but in the end they have all been part of my growth. None of this, I can tell, is very status quo, but it *is* authentic. And for me, owning my truth and honoring my deep desire to live life on my own terms is how it has to be. As Forrest Gump's momma used to say, "Life is a like a box of chocolates . . . you never know what you're gonna' get."

ENLIGHTENMENT IS SEXY CHAPTER TOOLBOX

Signs of Spiritual Awakening

Embrace the changes you are going through.
Resistance is the enemy.

Let go. Don't hold on to your old ways. They are
gone. Look to the future and don't look back.

Exercise and eat right.
You want your body working with you.

18

I Know What Sadness Is: Getting Perspective on Grief and Loss

"For a star to be born,
there is one thing that must happen:
a gaseous nebula must collapse.
So collapse.
Crumble.
This is not your destruction.
This is your birth."

—*Noor Tagori*

I am no stranger to sadness and depression. From a bad breakup to the death of a loved one, to just feeling badly, I have been there many times. However, through a lot of study, reflection and the experience of reconnecting to a more empowered sense of myself, I've found there *are* steps I can take and attitudes I can hold to smooth the way going forward, from grief to a renewed sense of deep appreciation for my life.

I can remember one time many years ago when I was dating a man who was completely wrong for me. (We've all been there, right?) My primary concern at that time was whether he was going to take me out on Saturday night. Putting that down on paper makes me laugh. I mean, really, get a life! But, I was madly in love with him. Never mind that many signs pointed in the direction of: *This Guy Isn't Right for You* and *He's Not Acting Like a Boyfriend Should.* They do say, "Love is blind" for a reason, right? Anyway, he broke up with me, virtually out of the blue, without any solid reasoning. I felt confused—blindsided by his decision—and completely out of control.

At the same time, I was devastated. Sadness paralyzed me. I felt like the world was ending. For a couple of months, I "worked it" to overcome my grief: I went to a therapist each week (I didn't want to repeat the same mistake and end up going down "Bad Breakup Road" again), talked to my friends for hours, started hanging out with different groups of people, worked out every day and lost 20 pounds. I began to love myself again, in the way I had long wanted *him* to love me.

I started to see our breakup had forced me to take a "time out," to really examine my life in a way that simply would not have been possible had I stayed with him. And I was glad for that. *Really* glad.

The point of this little story of woe? Obviously, my sadness was caused by my not getting what I wanted . . . but would I really have been so fulfilled if I'd *stayed* in that relationship? Oftentimes, getting to the other side of sadness (either kicking and screaming or through "letting go and letting God") is a land of new opportunities and much deeper satisfaction and joy.

What do you think happened next? Well, the Universe rewarded me handsomely—pun intended—with a new man, a man who respected and appreciated me more fully. How did *that* happen? I believe it was because I had done enough "homework" to get my focus back on taking care of and respecting myself, making smarter and healthier choices. And by doing so, I attracted to me a more satisfying, rewarding relationship.

In the past, I didn't want to see how wrong Guy #1 was for me, because I was dead-set on having my life turn out the way I thought it "should" (according to my ego-driven "perfect plan"). I didn't factor into the equation the importance of treating myself with respect, care and love. As a result, the Universe ever so kindly slammed the door in my face. And although I did go through a period of some uncomfortable growth (that's putting it mildly)—holy-moly, did I grow!—I eventually found the happiness within me again. (New man or no new man.)

Sadness sometimes becomes serious, though. And we don't always know how to handle it. When my mother passed away, I felt a sense of sadness deep within me that became extremely dangerous. I became so depressed that suicide seemed like the only logical option. However, through finding myself a great doctor, staying with my practice of meditation, and taking sufficient time for healing, I found my way out of it. I have no doubt that, in the process, I received a miracle. The key to my miracle, I believe, was the fact that I completely surrendered. I allowed sadness to exist without my resistance . . . and yes, it broke me in pieces. But looking back now, through the lens of time, I can see clearly, it was a gift.

The experience of my mom's passing, as painful as it was, taught me to pray like I had never prayed before. On one particularly sad evening, I went into my shower and just got on my hands and knees. I had been crying for days. There was nothing left in me. In my mind, I was already dead. I can remember the water pounding on my body as I began to completely unravel. In that moment, everything I had ever known became irrelevant in my life. I knew NOTHING . . . and I let go completely. I absolutely relinquished the idea that I was separate from God and the Universe. I knew that I either had to be carried to the other side of sadness or I was going to be dead. My mind, my thoughts, my learned "rules" about how I thought things should be, all died that morning on my shower floor. They went right down the drain with my tears. I screamed out, "Please, God, Mom, anyone who is listening! Please, I beg you, give me the strength to kill myself or a way out of this pain! I am completely in your hands. I am nothing! I surrender."

But after learning to meditate (T.M.), within two weeks, I was happier than I had ever been in my life.

Now, I'll agree the sadness and grief I'm describing here was pretty extreme. But the point is, the results I got from feeling my sadness and then surrendering it, from letting go of what I thought *needed to be happening* and trusting in something greater than me to guide me forward (God, the Universe), *that's* what allowed for my sadness to be healed and for something new to take its place.

These days, whenever I feel sadness creeping in on me, a bell rings in my mind. *Pay attention, it's time to make a change.* DING! DING! DING! I am willing to allow the sadness to move right through me. I no longer let it get to the point where

I'm thinking about drinking a bottle of bleach. It doesn't have to get that crazy. I've learned I don't get to choose everything in this world, but I *do* get to choose my mood. Yes indeed, we *can* be responsible for our decisions, as well as our actions. We *can* decide that life is magical and that we're going to *really live*. That decision *alone* can connect us back to happiness and blast away the sadness.

So, before sadness has you by the neck, look to see how God/the Universe may be guiding you and in what direction. Ask yourself, *What am I paying attention to?* Is there something new waiting for you around the bend? I've come to find what works for me is this: once I sense it's time to move forward from whatever sadness or grief I've been feeling, I just decide to open myself up to embrace the mysteries life has to offer (I see them as little pockets of magic). The following are a few concrete examples of possible action steps. Take a random road trip and discover there are areas of a not-too-distant city you naturally love. Upon meeting a stranger, keep open to what he or she has to say—it may be that he/she tells you something you needed to hear at that exact moment. Or upon hearing a new song on the radio, listen more carefully to the lyrics—to determine if they're speaking directly to you. It's all magic.

As you start to recognize when the Universe is winking at you, the world begins to twinkle. You start looking for the good, and unconsciously avoiding the bad. Doing what isn't good for you will no longer make sense. You move forward naturally, towards light, life and love.

Waves of sadness may come and go. Being real with our feelings and choosing to let them pass through us enables us to handle the ups and downs in life better and better. These days, I regularly check in with myself, monitoring how I am feeling. It's totally automatic now. It took a lot of work on myself to get to this point, but my motivation has never wavered. So now, no matter what the situation is, I disconnect from the outcome (i.e., trying to control it). My opinion of how things should look and eventually turn out just isn't that important—my happiness, however, is.

Ultimately, I've found that squarely facing and consciously "processing" the experience of sadness or pain can be one of the most powerful ways to help you grow, to reflect back to you something about the depth of your character, strength, adaptability and fortitude, like nothing else can.

My mom always told me, "Val, the bad never stays bad forever." She was right. It NEVER, EVER *stays* bad. I know this truth, now, and it makes a big difference in how I handle things that pop up in my life.

When a saddening occasion arises, be sad. Feel it. Own it. Walk right into the pain. Look at it dead in the eye. Let the sadness move you, let yourself grieve. You *can* get through it, overcome it. When you start saying to yourself, "I can't handle this," STOP. What is it you *can't* handle? What *can* you change so you can, not only handle it, but also grow in it . . . toward the person you were meant to be? Then, take one step in that direction – one step ahead of the sadness.

ENLIGHTENMENT IS SEXY CHAPTER TOOLBOX

I Know What Sadness Is

Pay attention to whatever emotion you're experiencing, resisting the temptation to ignore, judge, stuff or medicate your feelings.

Let the sadness have a place in you— don't avoid it.

Then, face your sadness, own it, and let it run its course.

As soon as you feel able to, choose happiness and take whatever steps you can to get back to embracing it daily. (And by all means, seek professional help/counseling, if necessary.)

19

Experience is Your Best Teacher

"Don't be satisfied with stories, how things have gone with others. Unfold your own myth."

—Rumi

Stop . . . listen . . . and repeat after me: *"We must learn from our own experience."*

I regularly read a lot—fiction and non-fiction, wildly diverse topics—and I'm certain I'll be learning forever. But nothing has prepared me more for this moment than *the experiences that led me here.* Getting knowledge from books is mostly intellectual and often theoretical. To really learn something, we need to *experience* it . . . we need to feel it. And the mind itself knows little of feeling.

When I decided I wanted to become a life coach, I thought, *Okay, I'll go to life coaching school.* It cost me about 8 grand, and I started . . . but one month into it, I knew I had made a HUGE error. The way they were instructing the students was based on knowledge I didn't agree with. We were told to "push" clients and make them "accountable" for their actions. Whoa, whoa, whoa! This was not going to work for me. This "corporate style" education was preaching a message in direct opposition to how I wanted to interact with my clients. I intuitively knew that if my clients were going to change, it was going to be on *their* terms and from the inside out. These "rules" my coaching school was handing out felt wrong to me, and there was no way I was going to use this format. I was worried for a couple of days, thinking, *How can I be a good life coach with no formal education? Would anyone take me seriously?*

Then I got quiet and opened myself up to the possibility of receiving some guidance. Almost immediately I had the thought, *Why do I have to follow someone else's model? Who the hell made that rule up?*

I knew who I was and what I believed in, and that I could help people—I'd known for decades I was just born with that gift. Ironically, I soon realized the essence of life coaching wasn't something that could readily be taught in school. I decided my time would be much better spent by just jumping in with two feet. I got myself a life coach who I believed in, and worked with him weekly, getting one-on-one lessons about how to be successful, not only financially, but how to empower my clients to become successful.

When I look back on that experience, I know it was a costly error, but you know what would have been worse? Wasting eight months of my life doing something I *knew* was wrong for me!

The moral of the story? Education is extremely important, but it can never take the place of experience. *Never.* Ideally, it is best to have both *and* to always be aware that real growth comes from getting your hands dirty. Meeting different people, connecting with them, seeing the world and trying different things. It will push you forward in your life, expand your horizons and break down the boundaries in your mind. You will know for YOURSELF what works for you. Not someone else's system, YOUR system. Designed completely by YOU.

Place confidence in your own experiences. Your own inner knowing, that gut feeling. Everything else, take with a grain of salt. How else are you really going to know? Where did the information come from? Who is relaying the goods? Is there any bias floating around? Any information you take in, choose to measure it with your own internal knowing. Don't rely on someone else's filter.

I can remember sitting in school and totally being uninterested. It didn't make any sense to me, having 6 classes a day, hopping from topic to topic like a frog. Never, not once in all my years of schooling until college, did anyone ever ask me what I was interested in learning, how I learned best or what really got me jazzed up. It was just a long, drawn-out series of sessions focused on information memorization and then barfing back up that information on a test . . . and then forgetting everything I just learned, *because it meant nothing to me.*

The teachers seemed like zombies to me, the "knowledge" given to me felt flat, and in the end, it was a horrible way to learn. Thank Jesus I had a mother who recognized who I was and gave me the gift of allowing me to just do okay in school . . . even if that meant coming home and reading about the *real* stuff that interested me. By 6th grade, I was devouring books on spirituality and mysticism with weekly trips to the metaphysical bookstore and public library with my mom. She also took me to plays, churches, museums and any other cultural or spiritual events I wanted to do (for example, going to see and meet Mother Teresa). My mom also taught me by just living and allowing me to move towards information that I was naturally drawn to. *And look where I am now?* I've been studying spirituality since I was 12. No classroom was going to give me that kind of education.

I'd like you to reflect for a few moments on how you feel when you get your information *on your own terms.* Do you feel more solid in your convictions, in your "knowing?"

You *and only you* can know your own truth. You find that through experience. "Self-knowledge" (as opposed to discovering "what to do" that suits YOU best regarding the circumstances you face in the world) can be gained, anytime at all, by taking a trip inside yourself and looking around with innocent eyes . . . that is, no false notions of what "should" be . . . just you exploring you.

Never let go of your childlike wonder. This keeps you innocent and non-judgmental. When you come from a pure space, you are like a sponge, able to soak up tons of knowledge. You are curious and tend to dig deeper into the different layers of an idea or viewpoint. Then you can ask yourself, *Where did that person's angle come from?* If it doesn't resonate with you, it's not *for* you. You are being handed someone *else's* understanding of an idea, which doesn't provide you with true understanding. It only encourages you to walk down the road of sheep, and we are not sheep!

Force nothing. When you are connected to life, everything just flows to you. You begin to know this when you dance with the Universe. You begin to understand you are being shown things for a reason. Ideas come to you for a higher purpose. Trust that everything is as it should be. You are cradled in the hands of the Universe. There are forces leading you to greatness, hoping you will "graduate." The world is your true classroom and your senses are your teachers. Listen to them, obey them and respect them.

Can you imagine what life would feel like just to be happy to be alive? Forget all the bullshit "things" that can be had from living in today's society. I mean just the basic feeling of *being human*. I've found it takes some getting used to, and it's likely you would to, since we've been programmed to always think with the mind. To always be taking action. Planning, plotting and always, *always* be going somewhere.

I decided I was going to just *be*. Nothing more and nothing less. I had zero interest in my future. I just wanted to focus on the "now." There were months and months that went by during which I just walked outside or took long drives. Just soaking in life and everything it had to offer. On the outside, it might have seemed like I was just wasting time, but the reality was I was setting the stage for the rest of my life. I was really taking the time to get to know myself and understand my relationship to every living thing around me. Each footstep I took outdoors, each mile driven with the windows opened, I was simply so happy to be a part of this world . . . and I felt every bird and every tree was my friend.

It might sound crazy, but those were some of the most precious days of my life. Simply being awake and healthy was enough for me, and it brought me so much happiness I thought my heart might explode. Each moment, so simple and so pure . . . experiencing a sense that my interior life was totally powerful and nothing on the outside had ever brought me that much joy. It's clear to me now I was experiencing the life force that runs though everyone and everything . . . teaching me things I could have *never* learned from anyone else.

Nature, the Universe itself was teaching me how to live and how to follow my destiny. In school classrooms, I was always being encouraged to "learn" new things and then regurgitate them on paper-and-pencil tests for "points." Um, yeah, that didn't work for me anymore. *Learning from experience* doesn't roll that way. You get to make up the rules and use your own filters. Every day is a chance for a new beginning, an opportunity to unlearn your old beliefs and expand. That sure sounds a hell of a lot better than sitting in a classroom eight hours a day memorizing information I likely will never use. Or following a set of rules that were made up by another person.

Listen up! We are strong women, *more* than capable of making our own rules. We are wise enough to let the Universe guide us and be our "true" teacher. Our personal guru. Who or what else knows more than God?

ENLIGHTENMENT IS SEXY CHAPTER TOOLBOX

Experience Is Your Best Teacher

Let "living" be your teacher.

Follow your OWN rules!

Hold on to your childlike wonder—take action each day to keep it alive in your awareness.

The Universe is here to teach us—
allow it to do just that.

20

What To Do When the World Doesn't Get You

"The only way to deal with an unfree world is to become so absolutely free that your very existence is an act of rebellion."

—*Albert Camus*

At the core, we all want to be accepted and loved. These needs are basic to our human nature. But this is the deal: if you are "different" or "sensitive" (empathic), the world is probably not going to always "get" you. Is that a problem? If so, there's support, encouraging words, attitude adjustments and suggested actions steps that can be found in the pages of this book for you. If not, great! Just keep on keepin' on!

I was born a highly sensitive person. It's been that way since day one. One of my first memories as a child, I think, was telling. It was a Monday morning, and I was standing at the top of the stairs that led down to my parent's basement. At the bottom of the stairs was my mom, folding some laundry. Simultaneously screaming and crying, I begged her not to send me to pre-school. The horror I felt inside, knowing I would have to be separated from her for half of the day and put in the care of people who I didn't know was way too heavy for me. Of course she was concerned about the trauma I was facing, and so tried to console me, but to no avail. Eventually, though, she got me to accept I would have to go to school. It took me an extremely long time to adjust to being away from her. Almost daily, for weeks, the school called her because I would not stop sobbing.

Thank God, for my sake, I had a parent who understood I was simply different. Being an "original" in my house was not a bad thing, but a good thing. I confided my troubles to my mom, and explained why I had such a difficult time concentrating in school. I told her I would walk into a room and "feel" the people around me. Sometimes it seemed like I was reading people's minds. Information I knew was privy only to this or that person somehow mysteriously downloaded to my brain. I would sit in the classroom and be completely overwhelmed by the information about the kids around me that flooded my mind. I could feel both their pain and happiness, and I had asked to feel neither. It was insane, and at times I felt like I was going mad.

Even though she didn't completely understand, my mom could empathize enough to support me. Always telling me to follow my own path and sup- porting me in my being different, she encouraged my individuality . . . *which is what I'm wanting to encourage in you!*

The main point is that I felt *different*, which you may very likely be able to identify with. My "dif- ference" was being empathic at a young age, but maybe yours was/is having bright red hair or being super-smart or talking with a lisp or being shorter or taller or skinnier or fatter than most. Sure, what- ever sets you apart from others *can* end up being something for which you're ridiculed . . . *or* you eventually discover—as I did—what makes a person different *can* become what makes them awesome!

This whole book, I hope you realize, is an alternative to the living "the status quo" – it's about living differently... since the world has so few support mechanisms for embracing and celebrating your uniqueness. I want people everywhere to know this is wrong, and encourage people to appreciate their own unique gifts and characteristics, no matter how strange or unlike others you are. Your differences from others are what make you able to offer this world something that no one else can.

To finish off with my story, as soon as I got older and moved out into the world, I realized other people didn't see me and my originality the way my mother did. Inwardly, I was deeply spiritual, while outwardly, I was extremely social. I never missed a dance or a party and I *always* had plans. But I kept my inner world between my mom and I, because I had tested the waters and could see I was getting serious negative feedback: "Val's so weird" or "Her ideas are crazy" or "She's so unrealistic."

At the same time, I sensed people really liked me. But *now* I can see they liked me because of whatever authenticity I had cultivated. However, I wasn't being *truly* authentic, because I was scared, back then, about how people would react to me if I spilled the beans about this heavy-duty intuition that was streaming through my veins.

Naturally, I began censoring myself around certain people, essentially hiding who I was, not wanting to seem totally odd—since, as the opening line of this chapter says, I wanted to be accepted and loved. I also didn't want others to laugh at me.

At the end of the day, though, I always had my mom, who was perpetually enthusiastic and appreciative of my ideas. I can see now she was a profound gift to me. She, too, was "different," so she got it. It wasn't until she died and I broke down, then recovered (in spades), that I felt committed to being myself, regardless of the circumstances. Then, the thought of being anyone other than my true self was simply out of the question.

As soon as I started meditating and diving deep down into my soul twice a day, the floodgates of my true self flew open. I started writing about spirituality, talking to friends about how we could change the world, and explaining how I wanted to do things differently. The system I saw around me seemed broken, and I felt inspired to figure out a way to make it better. For me, this book is one important step in that direction.

As I mentioned before, I lost some friends. They could not handle this "new" person who was actually always there—the dormant part of me who was now ready to bloom. So what did I do? I made new friends, who not only understood me, but actually *fueled* my soul. They made me feel loved and totally accepted. This felt like a long-awaited miracle.

I began to understand that being different is actually a blessing. There is no one else in the world exactly like you. Thank God. We are born with a set of talents and gifts and characteristics that are uniquely ours, a distinctive sum of parts that make up the extraordinary, truly special whole of who we are. And by the way: *the world needs each of us . . . and* our ideas, dreams and visions (even if some get labeled "wacky" along the way).

What the world does *not* need is another robot just moving along, doing exactly as it's told. Think about it: who are the most interesting people in history? *The people who followed their own sense of truth.* Those who went on to show the world a better way and carved out a better path for us to walk upon. Almost always, these people are viewed as the troublemakers and the rebels. The people who make history are those who *embrace* their own eccentricities and live authentically, encouraging— not discouraging—unconventionality.

When I meet truly authentic humans, they typically blow me away! They're like a breath of fresh air . . . the opposite of sheep. This lesson is so important, and yet I know it can be hard. Every day, we're being herded toward a box. Society seems to *constantly* remind us how we "should" do things. Sure, it can be scary to go against the grain, to stand on your own and disagree with a lot of the structures that are in place for people to follow. I would never say it was easy, but in the end it is *always* worth it to be true to who you really are.

This commitment to showing up authentically—regardless of whether the world "gets" you or not—is one of the keys to living from that place of inner knowing, the wiser part of you that knows your unique gifts and innate value to the world . . . *and* intuitively understands what is right for YOU. Not your sister, not your neighbor, but YOU. When you get lined up with that, just your presence will be enough to inspire the people around you to be *their* authentic selves.

When we unplug from the approval of other people and institutions, we plug into Nature, into the Universe, into God. People and things can't be relied upon to nurture this feeling we all occasionally have inside. For that, you have to connect with something much greater to: a) give you strength to be your true self and b) lead you, guide you to your highest, truest self.

Somewhere along the way, the vast majority of us forgot or lost track of who we truly are. Usually what came next was a whole bunch of pain to shake us down and make us question everything we thought we knew, in order to see the real meaning of our lives. Taking a new course, commencing upon a new journey to reclaim and live one's most authentic self every day, in every instance, this is one of the greatest decisions a person can make.

So I say, be defiant. Be *extremely* defiant to a society that so often tells you the opposite of what is true. Allow yourself to feel, *really* feel what is happening around you. Start to understand *your* reality, not someone else's version of it or their opinion of how your life should be. Set to the side your ego's voice, because it is the voice that says you are separate from everything and will never have enough. It is the voice of "the small self." What we are going after is the Big Self, the High Self . . . the Self that KNOWS we are connected to everything . . . the Self that IS love. Once you embrace that undeniable sense of yourself, you are on the high road, and the Universe will move mountains for you.

ENLIGHTENMENT IS SEXY CHAPTER TOOLBOX

What to Do When the World Doesn't Get You

Embrace your uniqueness.

Surround yourself with people
who can actually "see" you.

Don't follow the pack.

Connect to your "higher self" through a
spiritual practice that suits *you*, and
leave behind your "small self."

21

The Misunderstood Power of Prayer

"The function of prayer is not to influence God, but rather to change the nature of the one who prays."

—Soren Kierkegaard

Introductory Note: Realizing society generally regards "prayer" as a very personal matter, I'm going to share (in this chapter) what my experience is and what works for me. If something I express here can be useful to you, great! If not, please take nothing here personally.

I live in a state of continuous prayer, a never-ending conversation with God/the Universe, which is always lighting my path, teaching me about my limits and my unlimited-ness, and showing me how to live a life of greater freedom, service and joy. What I think is important is the *way* I pray. Contrary to the norm, I don't ask for things. Instead, I tell God I'm open to His plan. His dreams are my dreams, His desires are my desires. Like Mother Teresa said, "Prayer is not asking. Prayer is putting oneself in the hands of God, at His disposition, and listening to His voice in the depth of our hearts."

I suggest trying this approach to prayer: "I am nothing but a vessel for God's love and God's purpose for me." Variations on this are the only way I pray now. If God decided I'd be doing the highest good as a house maid or a country's queen, it would be the same to me. My trust doesn't waver.

Adopting this attitude has changed my life and put people and situations on my path that have absolutely filled me with joy and insight. It seems like every day, I meet people who can help me on my "life path." They come in the form of introductions, random meetings and pure serendipity. It's so obvious to me when this happens. I just have to laugh to myself.

Since God/the Universe doesn't have boundaries or limits, don't limit yourself. Every day, I simply pray, "Use me, work through me, show me what to do. I trust you, completely and always." And then I just listen and watch, keeping open to whatever guidance I'm offered. This accomplishes two things: 1) The pressure is off of me; and 2) I put my fate in God's hands. Anything IS possible in this state of affairs . . . and my life has been a testament to how true this is! Out-of-the-blue introductions to horizon-expanding people, serendipitous meetings, supportive gifts and opportunities all seem to line up for my "heart's wishes" to be fulfilled effortlessly! Wowza!

For me, prayer isn't about what I want or what you want, because I don't see God as Santa Claus, nor are we 5-year-olds with a list of toys we want for the holidays. This goes back to the idea that you are not in control. When one "gets" the value, the rightness of surrendering themselves to a higher power/God, prayer no longer is about what "I" feel I need. Prayer then turns into, "God show me what You want me to do. Where to go and how to live."

There will be points in all of our lives when we will be praying for "someone special" to come into our lives, or a miracle for a sick loved one, or even for help getting out of a jam. We are human, and we can't always be living in the "God, show me the way" space. But we are missing the point if we are praying to "get" something. My sense is that prayer shouldn't be about trying to change God's mind toward helping you or me out in precisely the way we think we'll be best served. Nope, I think the Universe/God has got things better handled and does not need me dictating terms. I mean, *really*.

So that leaves me believing prayer is at its best when it's about changing ourselves . . . seeking guidance, direction, ". . . and the power to carry it out." So yes, to me, turning to God in prayer for that guidance and assistance in whatever form seems like the most righteous use of prayer.

However, you might be saying, "If I pray enough, I will get the man of my dreams." Or "If I pray enough, God will help me win the lotto." This is ridiculous. I mean, since when did you come to KNOW what's best for you, cosmically speaking? I don't know one person, myself included, who has strategized their way into omniscience! My suggestion? We all consider praying that everything in creation will support us and show us the best way forward! God knows we are never going to figure it out on our own. To me, these personal "needs" seem to indicate a "disconnect" from one's Higher Power . . . a distraction from hearing the whispers from the Divine, the Cosmos.

But once you have come to a state of actual humility, once you've surrendered your pride and acknowledged you are not truly "self-sufficient" or "self-reliant" (nor do you need to try to be), prayer can become a constant, living reality. You can naturally start communicating with God/the Universe/ your Higher Power on a consistent basis.

What I'm proposing about prayer here very likely has NOTHING to do with what you were taught in your church, synagogue or mosque. Prayer, as I'm describing it here, is about having a constant union with the Universe/the Divine . . . being centered in the knowing that you are walking hand-in-hand with God. *Whoa, dude!* Sure doesn't sound like the Sunday School lessons *I* learned growing up.

This isn't about rules or being forced to "pray" or attend services. This is about transformation, shedding your ego, your "small self," and walking into the kind of radical grace only the Universe Itself/God can show you. It's the ultimate connection and it looks nothing like any connection any of us have experienced on an "earthly" level. When you hit this level of prayer, you know your life has completely changed. This "conscious contact" with the Universe, with God, isn't about belief . . . no, when you have a deep relationship with the Universe, you KNOW you are being listened to. And you can see evidence in your life every single day. It will be obvious and it will come from a knowing in your soul. This is the greatest gift we can ask for: personal guidance and transformation . . . toward the state of being truly free.

Actually, if our religious organizations *were* teaching us about direct contact with God, they'd probably be out of business pretty fast. The point is, many of us have found (or are finding) we don't "need" a middleman. We are born spiritual beings in a human body, and our goal is to just acknowledge that. That's it! *Come back home to ourselves.* It's so simple, that once you figure it out, it's mind blowing that something so natural seemed so far away. Having a daily, intimate relationship with the Divine/the Cosmos was inside of us the entire time.

So next time someone tells you the "rules" about getting into heaven or who you have to pray to or how you need to pray, you can tell them with confidence, "Thanks, but no thanks. I have a personal relationship with the Universe, and I know what I need to do."

None of us need to be trying to "get" anywhere. Close your eyes, take a deep breath, pray to be shown what to do and say, listen for the Universe's/God's response . . . and know you have arrived. Heaven on Earth, the Promised Land, Shangri-la or the Hogwarts School of Witchcraft and Wizardry. I don't care what you call it. Just let your prayer illumine you to your connection to God/the Universe and how to live . . . right here . . . right now.

ENLIGHTENMENT IS SEXY CHAPTER TOOLBOX

The Misunderstood Power of Prayer

Decide what prayer means to you,
not to anyone else.

Don't ask for "things" . . . instead, ask God/
the Universe/Spirit to use you
and work through you.

Consider how you can incorporate prayer
into your daily existence—that is,
more-or-less communing with God/
the Universe/Spirit throughout the day.

Make God/the Universe/Spirit your "main
man," who you turn to for-… well, everything.

22

Open Letter to You, Dear Reader

"We are all just walking each other home."

—*Ram Dass*

I'm not a guru or a spiritual know-it-all. I'm just a regular girl who had an amazing experience...and then it continued. I don't know everything, but what I do know I have shared with you. I don't expect you to follow me or do exactly as I say. My wish is that, just maybe, this book will make you question something/someone when it/he/she doesn't feel right to you. Or that you'll stay open to new perspectives and drink in all that comes your way, living as freely and creatively as humanly possible. If I have given you even a glimpse into that possibility, then I did something right.

I felt like you would just get it—it's why you would be drawn to this book—that river of truth running through all of us. If you listen, it will whisper in your ear . . . guiding you forward to, hopefully, a better road map for your life. Given your interest in this book's topics, very likely you're unusually intuitive, sensitive, caring and connected. These traits can be a double-edged sword, though: sure, you *know* things and when you quiet your mind, you really *feel* the world. On the other hand, most of the world isn't operating at that level, so you may often feel misunderstood or "different." That's actually why I wrote this book. To help you understand you're not only different, you are *the exception to the rule.* The free thinker, the rebel, the renegade. And that's a *gift!* You are among the women who are going to change the world. *Enlightenment is*

Sexy is a direct acknowledgment of your uniqueness and a trumpet-call for your dreams. You *can* be different. You *can* make a difference. And you *can* be happy. *Every day.*

You are a light in a world that can sometimes feel quite dark. You are a seeker *and* a knower of reality... and an example of deep love. Keep on your individual path. Live from your gut. Listen to your soul. You are being led by invisible forces that will give you an amazing life. All you have to do is listen.

Dedication & Acknowledgment

DEDICATION

This book is dedicated to the most unique, wildly talented and loving mother a girl could ask for, my mom, Patricia Kelly Gangas. She showed me what it means to be a child of God through her endless generosity, kindness without boundaries and unshakable faith. Mom, I love you today, tomorrow and forever. Oh, and if you were wondering if I'm picking up on all your signs (Fire & Rain) and listening to you when you talk to me in my dreams, I am. Keep it up!

xoxo,
Monkeyface

ACKNOWLEDGEMENT

To my kick-ass editor, Willy Mathes, without whom this book would not be possible. (I mean, it's so true! Let's be real!) And to every person (there are too many to name) who believed in my vision, who slipped me a couple of bucks to make my dream a reality, and who stood by all my crazy ideas, thank you. You boosted my strength & faith to just go for it… BOOM!